Cookies

Recipes to make your own gifts

Use these recipes to delight your friends and family. Each recipe includes gift tags for your convenience — just cut them out and personalize!

To decorate jars, cut fabric in 9" diameter circles. Screw down the jar ring to hold fabric in place or hold fabric with a ribbon, raffia, twine, yarn, lace, or string (first secure the fabric with a rubber band before tying). Punch a hole into the corner of the tag and use the ribbon, raffia, twine, yarn, lace, or string to attach the tag to the jar.

These gifts should keep for up to six months. If the mix contains nuts, it should be used within three months.

Printed in the United States of America
by G&R Publishing Co.

Second Edition

Distributed By:

507 Industrial Street
Waverly, IA 50677

ISBN 1-56383-121-X
Item #3001

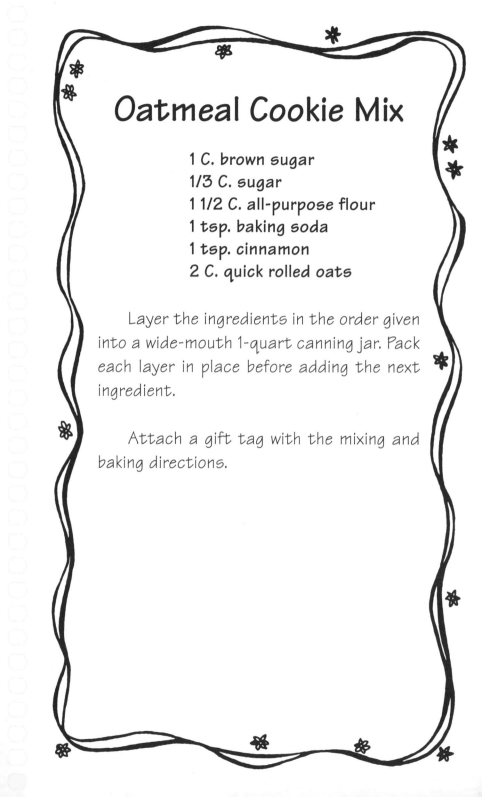

Oatmeal Cookie Mix

1 C. brown sugar
1/3 C. sugar
1 1/2 C. all-purpose flour
1 tsp. baking soda
1 tsp. cinnamon
2 C. quick rolled oats

Layer the ingredients in the order given into a wide-mouth 1-quart canning jar. Pack each layer in place before adding the next ingredient.

Attach a gift tag with the mixing and baking directions.

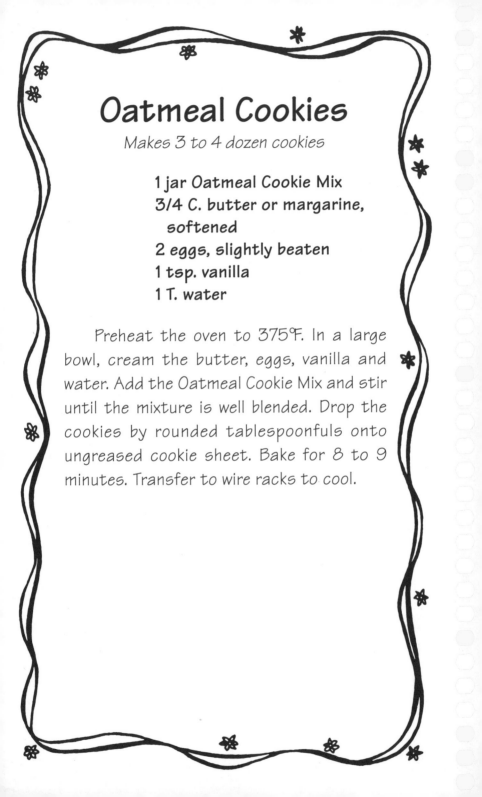

Oatmeal Cookies

Makes 3 to 4 dozen cookies

1 jar Oatmeal Cookie Mix
3/4 C. butter or margarine,
   softened
2 eggs, slightly beaten
1 tsp. vanilla
1 T. water

Preheat the oven to 375°F. In a large bowl, cream the butter, eggs, vanilla and water. Add the Oatmeal Cookie Mix and stir until the mixture is well blended. Drop the cookies by rounded tablespoonfuls onto ungreased cookie sheet. Bake for 8 to 9 minutes. Transfer to wire racks to cool.

Oatmeal Cookies
Makes 3 to 4 dozen cookies

1 jar Oatmeal Cookie Mix
3/4 C. butter or margarine,
  softened

2 eggs, slightly beaten
1 tsp. vanilla
1 T. water

Preheat the oven to 375°F. In a large bowl, cream the butter, eggs, vanilla and water. Add the Oatmeal Cookie Mix and stir until the mixture is well blended. Drop the cookies by rounded tablespoonfuls onto ungreased cookie sheet. Bake for 8 to 9 minutes. Transfer to wire racks to cool.

Oatmeal Cookies
Makes 3 to 4 dozen cookies

1 jar Oatmeal Cookie Mix
3/4 C. butter or margarine,
  softened

2 eggs, slightly beaten
1 tsp. vanilla
1 T. water

Preheat the oven to 375°F. In a large bowl, cream the butter, eggs, vanilla and water. Add the Oatmeal Cookie Mix and stir until the mixture is well blended. Drop the cookies by rounded tablespoonfuls onto ungreased cookie sheet. Bake for 8 to 9 minutes. Transfer to wire racks to cool.

Oatmeal Cookies
Makes 3 to 4 dozen cookies

1 jar Oatmeal Cookie Mix
3/4 C. butter or margarine,
  softened

2 eggs, slightly beaten
1 tsp. vanilla
1 T. water

Preheat the oven to 375°F. In a large bowl, cream the butter, eggs, vanilla and water. Add the Oatmeal Cookie Mix and stir until the mixture is well blended. Drop the cookies by rounded tablespoonfuls onto ungreased cookie sheet. Bake for 8 to 9 minutes. Transfer to wire racks to cool.

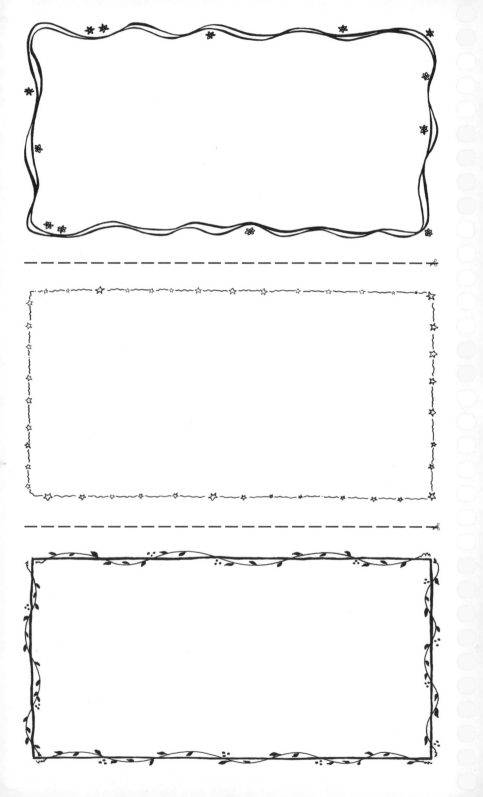

Oatmeal Cookies
Makes 3 to 4 dozen cookies

1 jar Oatmeal Cookie Mix
3/4 C. butter or margarine,
  softened

2 eggs, slightly beaten
1 tsp. vanilla
1 T. water

Preheat the oven to 375°F. In a large bowl, cream the butter, eggs, vanilla and water. Add the Oatmeal Cookie Mix and stir until the mixture is well blended. Drop the cookies by rounded tablespoonfuls onto ungreased cookie sheet. Bake for 8 to 9 minutes. Transfer to wire racks to cool.

Oatmeal Cookies
Makes 3 to 4 dozen cookies

1 jar Oatmeal Cookie Mix
3/4 C. butter or margarine,
  softened

2 eggs, slightly beaten
1 tsp. vanilla
1 T. water

Preheat the oven to 375°F. In a large bowl, cream the butter, eggs, vanilla and water. Add the Oatmeal Cookie Mix and stir until the mixture is well blended. Drop the cookies by rounded tablespoonfuls onto ungreased cookie sheet. Bake for 8 to 9 minutes. Transfer to wire racks to cool.

Oatmeal Cookies
Makes 3 to 4 dozen cookies

1 jar Oatmeal Cookie Mix
3/4 C. butter or margarine,
  softened

2 eggs, slightly beaten
1 tsp. vanilla
1 T. water

Preheat the oven to 375°F. In a large bowl, cream the butter, eggs, vanilla and water. Add the Oatmeal Cookie Mix and stir until the mixture is well blended. Drop the cookies by rounded tablespoonfuls onto ungreased cookie sheet. Bake for 8 to 9 minutes. Transfer to wire racks to cool.

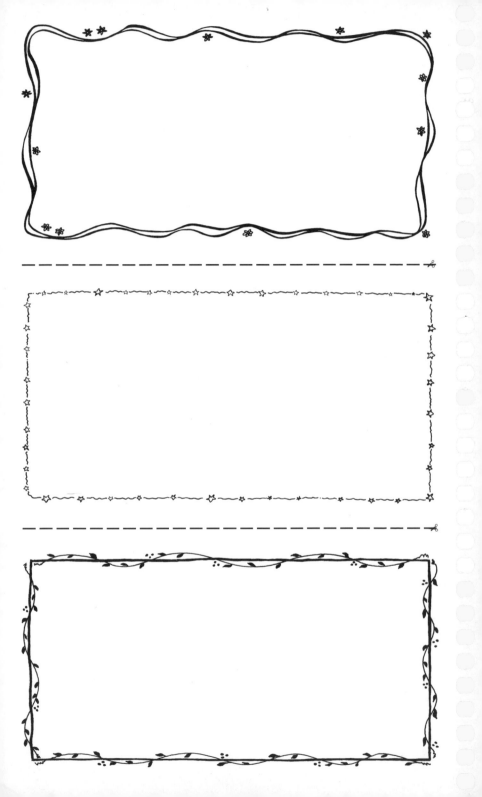

Snickerdoodle Cookie Mix

2 3/4 C. all-purpose flour
1/4 tsp. salt
1 tsp. baking soda
2 tsp. cream of tartar
1 1/2 C. sugar

Layer the ingredients in the order given into a wide-mouth 1-quart canning jar. Pack each layer in place before adding the next ingredient.

Attach a gift tag with the mixing and baking directions.

Snickerdoodles

Makes 4 to 5 dozen cookies

1 jar Snickerdoodle Cookie Mix
1 C. butter or margarine,
   softened
2 eggs, slightly beaten
1/2 C. sugar
1 T. cinnamon

Preheat the oven to 375°F. In a large bowl, cream the butter until light, add the eggs and beat, until the mixture is smooth. Add the Snickerdoodle Cookie Mix and continue to beat until the dough begins to form. Combine the sugar and cinnamon in a small bowl. Shape the dough into 1-inch balls and roll in the cinnamon-sugar blend. Arrange on ungreased cookie sheet and bake for 10 to 15 minutes or until light tan. Transfer to wire racks to cool.

Snickerdoodles
Makes 4 to 5 dozen cookies

1 jar Snickerdoodle Cookie Mix
1 C. butter or margarine,
  softened

2 eggs, slightly beaten
1/2 C. sugar
1 T. cinnamon

Preheat the oven to 375°F. In a large bowl, cream the butter until light, add the eggs and beat, until the mixture is smooth. Add the Snickerdoodle Cookie Mix and continue to beat until the dough begins to form. Combine the sugar and cinnamon in a small bowl. Shape the dough into 1-inch balls and roll in the cinnamon-sugar blend. Arrange on ungreased cookie sheet and bake for 10 to 15 minutes or until light tan. Transfer to wire racks to cool.

Snickerdoodles
Makes 4 to 5 dozen cookies

1 jar Snickerdoodle Cookie Mix
1 C. butter or margarine,
  softened

2 eggs, slightly beaten
1/2 C. sugar
1 T. cinnamon

Preheat the oven to 375°F. In a large bowl, cream the butter until light, add the eggs and beat, until the mixture is smooth. Add the Snickerdoodle Cookie Mix and continue to beat until the dough begins to form. Combine the sugar and cinnamon in a small bowl. Shape the dough into 1-inch balls and roll in the cinnamon-sugar blend. Arrange on ungreased cookie sheet and bake for 10 to 15 minutes or until light tan. Transfer to wire racks to cool.

Snickerdoodles
Makes 4 to 5 dozen cookies

1 jar Snickerdoodle Cookie Mix
1 C. butter or margarine,
  softened

2 eggs, slightly beaten
1/2 C. sugar
1 T. cinnamon

Preheat the oven to 375°F. In a large bowl, cream the butter until light, add the eggs and beat, until the mixture is smooth. Add the Snickerdoodle Cookie Mix and continue to beat until the dough begins to form. Combine the sugar and cinnamon in a small bowl. Shape the dough into 1-inch balls and roll in the cinnamon-sugar blend. Arrange on ungreased cookie sheet and bake for 10 to 15 minutes or until light tan. Transfer to wire racks to cool.

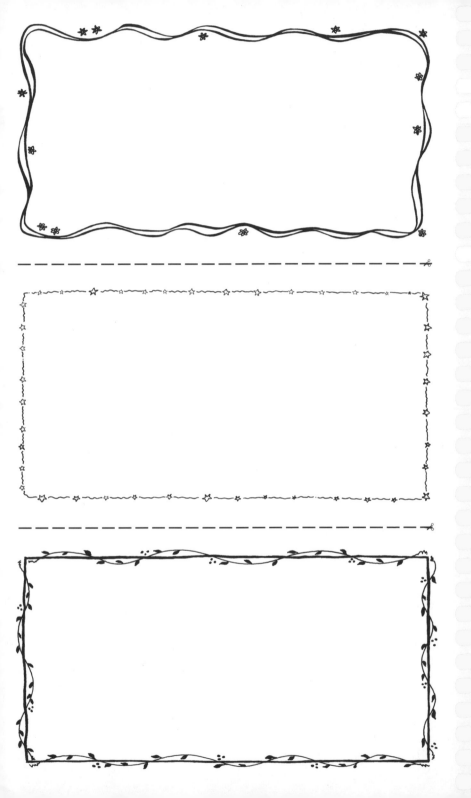

Snickerdoodles
Makes 4 to 5 dozen cookies

1 jar Snickerdoodle Cookie Mix
1 C. butter or margarine,
  softened

2 eggs, slightly beaten
1/2 C. sugar
1 T. cinnamon

Preheat the oven to 375°F. In a large bowl, cream the butter until light, add the eggs and beat, until the mixture is smooth. Add the Snickerdoodle Cookie Mix and continue to beat until the dough begins to form. Combine the sugar and cinnamon in a small bowl. Shape the dough into 1-inch balls and roll in the cinnamon-sugar blend. Arrange on ungreased cookie sheet and bake for 10 to 15 minutes or until light tan. Transfer to wire racks to cool.

Snickerdoodles
Makes 4 to 5 dozen cookies

1 jar Snickerdoodle Cookie Mix
1 C. butter or margarine,
  softened

2 eggs, slightly beaten
1/2 C. sugar
1 T. cinnamon

Preheat the oven to 375°F. In a large bowl, cream the butter until light, add the eggs and beat, until the mixture is smooth. Add the Snickerdoodle Cookie Mix and continue to beat until the dough begins to form. Combine the sugar and cinnamon in a small bowl. Shape the dough into 1-inch balls and roll in the cinnamon-sugar blend. Arrange on ungreased cookie sheet and bake for 10 to 15 minutes or until light tan. Transfer to wire racks to cool.

Snickerdoodles
Makes 4 to 5 dozen cookies

1 jar Snickerdoodle Cookie Mix
1 C. butter or margarine,
  softened

2 eggs, slightly beaten
1/2 C. sugar
1 T. cinnamon

Preheat the oven to 375°F. In a large bowl, cream the butter until light, add the eggs and beat, until the mixture is smooth. Add the Snickerdoodle Cookie Mix and continue to beat until the dough begins to form. Combine the sugar and cinnamon in a small bowl. Shape the dough into 1-inch balls and roll in the cinnamon-sugar blend. Arrange on ungreased cookie sheet and bake for 10 to 15 minutes or until light tan. Transfer to wire racks to cool.

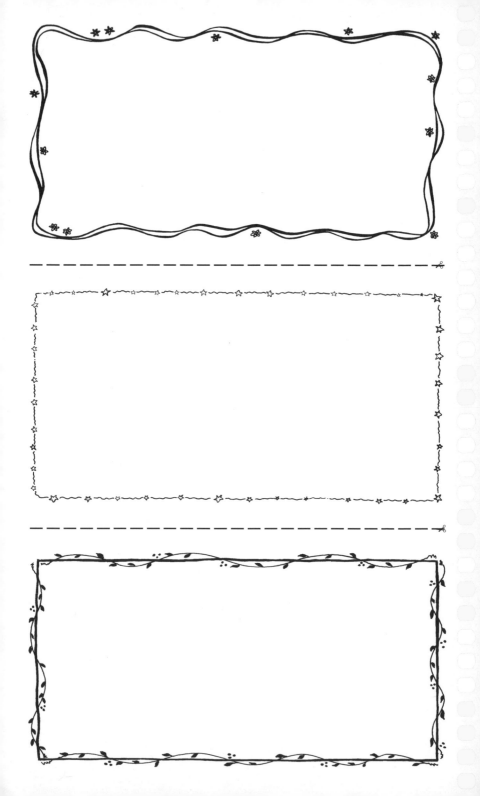

Chocolate Chip Cookie Mix

1 tsp. baking powder
1 tsp. baking soda
1/2 tsp. salt
3/4 C. all-purpose flour
1/4 C. sugar
1/4 C. brown sugar
1 C. chocolate chips
1/2 C. brown sugar
1/4 C. sugar
1 C. all-purpose flour

Layer the ingredients in the order given into a wide-mouth 1-quart canning jar. Pack each layer in place before adding the next ingredient.

Attach a gift tag with the mixing and baking directions.

Chocolate Chip Cookies

Makes 3 to 4 dozen cookies

1 jar Chocolate Chip Cookie Mix
3/4 C. butter or margarine,
 softened
2 eggs, slightly beaten
1/2 tsp. vanilla

Preheat the oven to 375°F. In a large bowl, cream the butter, eggs and vanilla. Add the Chocolate Chip Cookie Mix and stir until the mixture is well blended. Drop by rounded tablespoonfuls onto greased cookie sheet. Bake for 8 to 10 minutes. Transfer to wire racks to cool.

Chocolate Chip Cookies
Makes 3 to 4 dozen cookies

1 jar Chocolate Chip Cookie Mix
3/4 C. butter or margarine,
  softened

2 eggs, slightly beaten
1/2 tsp. vanilla

Preheat the oven to 375°F. In a large bowl, cream the butter, eggs and vanilla. Add the Chocolate Chip Cookie Mix and stir until the mixture is well blended. Drop by rounded tablespoonfuls onto greased cookie sheet. Bake for 8 to 10 minutes. Transfer to wire racks to cool.

Chocolate Chip Cookies
Makes 3 to 4 dozen cookies

1 jar Chocolate Chip Cookie Mix
3/4 C. butter or margarine,
  softened

2 eggs, slightly beaten
1/2 tsp. vanilla

Preheat the oven to 375°F. In a large bowl, cream the butter, eggs and vanilla. Add the Chocolate Chip Cookie Mix and stir until the mixture is well blended. Drop by rounded tablespoonfuls onto greased cookie sheet. Bake for 8 to 10 minutes. Transfer to wire racks to cool.

Chocolate Chip Cookies
Makes 3 to 4 dozen cookies

1 jar Chocolate Chip Cookie Mix
3/4 C. butter or margarine,
  softened

2 eggs, slightly beaten
1/2 tsp. vanilla

Preheat the oven to 375°F. In a large bowl, cream the butter, eggs and vanilla. Add the Chocolate Chip Cookie Mix and stir until the mixture is well blended. Drop by rounded tablespoonfuls onto greased cookie sheet. Bake for 8 to 10 minutes. Transfer to wire racks to cool.

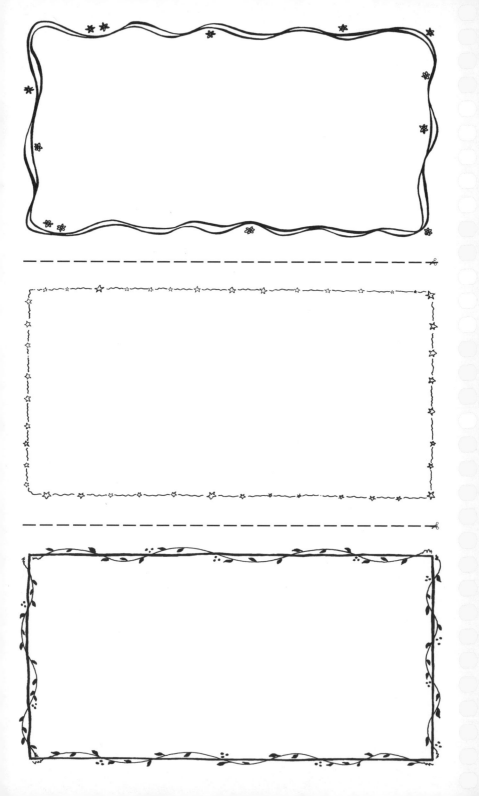

Chocolate Chip Cookies
Makes 3 to 4 dozen cookies

1 jar Chocolate Chip Cookie Mix
3/4 C. butter or margarine,
   softened

2 eggs, slightly beaten
1/2 tsp. vanilla

Preheat the oven to 375°F. In a large bowl, cream the butter, eggs and vanilla. Add the Chocolate Chip Cookie Mix and stir until the mixture is well blended. Drop by rounded tablespoonfuls onto greased cookie sheet. Bake for 8 to 10 minutes. Transfer to wire racks to cool.

Chocolate Chip Cookies
Makes 3 to 4 dozen cookies

1 jar Chocolate Chip Cookie Mix
3/4 C. butter or margarine,
   softened

2 eggs, slightly beaten
1/2 tsp. vanilla

Preheat the oven to 375°F. In a large bowl, cream the butter, eggs and vanilla. Add the Chocolate Chip Cookie Mix and stir until the mixture is well blended. Drop by rounded tablespoonfuls onto greased cookie sheet. Bake for 8 to 10 minutes. Transfer to wire racks to cool.

Chocolate Chip Cookies
Makes 3 to 4 dozen cookies

1 jar Chocolate Chip Cookie Mix
3/4 C. butter or margarine,
   softened

2 eggs, slightly beaten
1/2 tsp. vanilla

Preheat the oven to 375°F. In a large bowl, cream the butter, eggs and vanilla. Add the Chocolate Chip Cookie Mix and stir until the mixture is well blended. Drop by rounded tablespoonfuls onto greased cookie sheet. Bake for 8 to 10 minutes. Transfer to wire racks to cool.

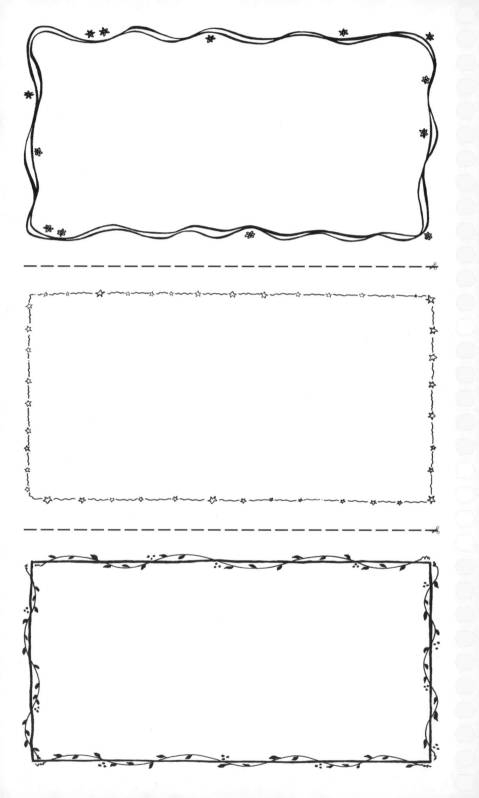

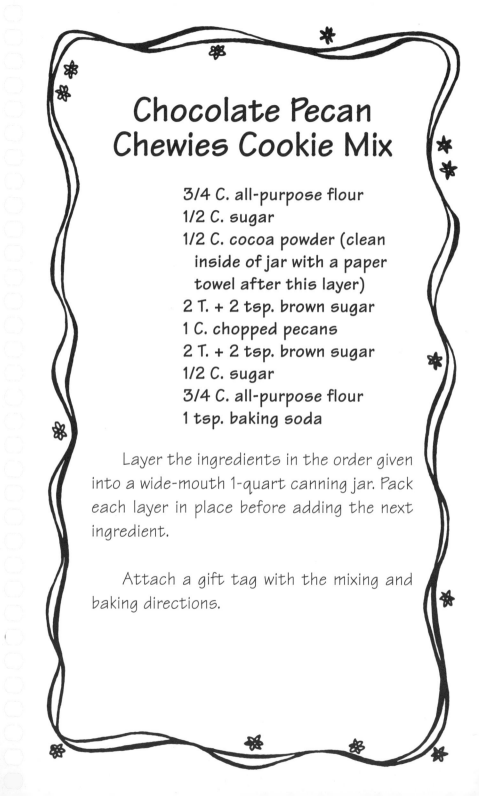

Chocolate Pecan Chewies Cookie Mix

3/4 C. all-purpose flour
1/2 C. sugar
1/2 C. cocoa powder (clean
  inside of jar with a paper
  towel after this layer)
2 T. + 2 tsp. brown sugar
1 C. chopped pecans
2 T. + 2 tsp. brown sugar
1/2 C. sugar
3/4 C. all-purpose flour
1 tsp. baking soda

Layer the ingredients in the order given into a wide-mouth 1-quart canning jar. Pack each layer in place before adding the next ingredient.

Attach a gift tag with the mixing and baking directions.

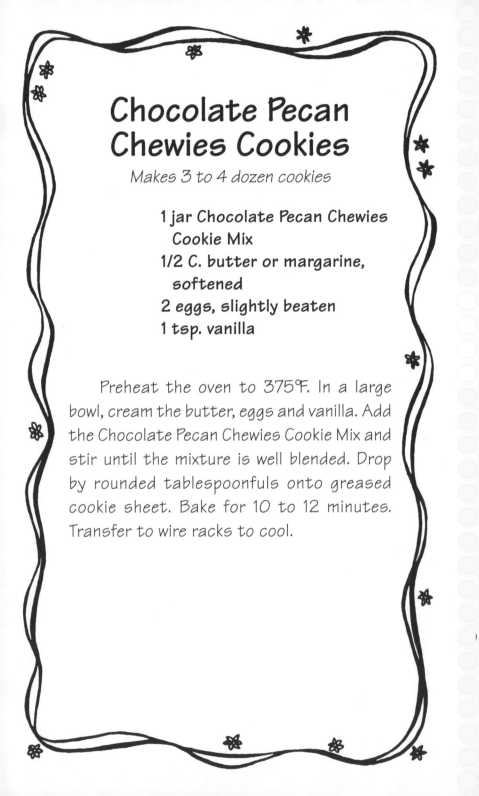

Chocolate Pecan Chewies Cookies

Makes 3 to 4 dozen cookies

1 jar Chocolate Pecan Chewies
  Cookie Mix
1/2 C. butter or margarine,
  softened
2 eggs, slightly beaten
1 tsp. vanilla

Preheat the oven to 375°F. In a large bowl, cream the butter, eggs and vanilla. Add the Chocolate Pecan Chewies Cookie Mix and stir until the mixture is well blended. Drop by rounded tablespoonfuls onto greased cookie sheet. Bake for 10 to 12 minutes. Transfer to wire racks to cool.

Chocolate Pecan Chewies Cookies
Makes 3 to 4 dozen cookies

1 jar Chocolate Pecan Chewies
  Cookie Mix
1/2 C. butter or margarine,
  softened

2 eggs, slightly beaten
1 tsp. vanilla

Preheat the oven to 375°F. In a large bowl, cream the butter, eggs and vanilla. Add the Chocolate Pecan Chewies Cookie Mix and stir until the mixture is well blended. Drop by rounded tablespoonfuls onto greased cookie sheet. Bake for 10 to 12 minutes. Transfer to wire racks to cool.

Chocolate Pecan Chewies Cookies
Makes 3 to 4 dozen cookies

1 jar Chocolate Pecan Chewies
  Cookie Mix
1/2 C. butter or margarine,
  softened

2 eggs, slightly beaten
1 tsp. vanilla

Preheat the oven to 375°F. In a large bowl, cream the butter, eggs and vanilla. Add the Chocolate Pecan Chewies Cookie Mix and stir until the mixture is well blended. Drop by rounded tablespoonfuls onto greased cookie sheet. Bake for 10 to 12 minutes. Transfer to wire racks to cool.

Chocolate Pecan Chewies Cookies
Makes 3 to 4 dozen cookies

1 jar Chocolate Pecan Chewies
  Cookie Mix
1/2 C. butter or margarine,
  softened

2 eggs, slightly beaten
1 tsp. vanilla

Preheat the oven to 375°F. In a large bowl, cream the butter, eggs and vanilla. Add the Chocolate Pecan Chewies Cookie Mix and stir until the mixture is well blended. Drop by rounded tablespoonfuls onto greased cookie sheet. Bake for 10 to 12 minutes. Transfer to wire racks to cool.

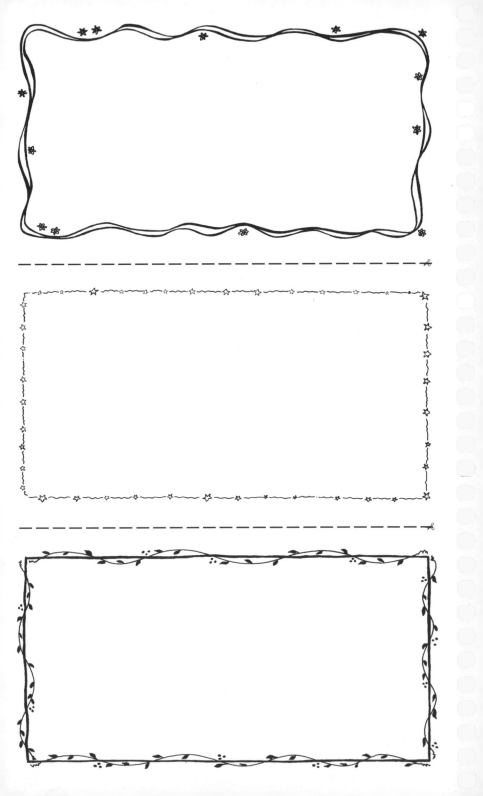

Chocolate Pecan Chewies Cookies
Makes 3 to 4 dozen cookies

1 jar Chocolate Pecan Chewies
  Cookie Mix
1/2 C. butter or margarine,
  softened

2 eggs, slightly beaten
1 tsp. vanilla

Preheat the oven to 375°F. In a large bowl, cream the butter, eggs and vanilla. Add the Chocolate Pecan Chewies Cookie Mix and stir until the mixture is well blended. Drop by rounded tablespoonfuls onto greased cookie sheet. Bake for 10 to 12 minutes. Transfer to wire racks to cool.

Chocolate Pecan Chewies Cookies
Makes 3 to 4 dozen cookies

1 jar Chocolate Pecan Chewies
  Cookie Mix
1/2 C. butter or margarine,
  softened

2 eggs, slightly beaten
1 tsp. vanilla

Preheat the oven to 375°F. In a large bowl, cream the butter, eggs and vanilla. Add the Chocolate Pecan Chewies Cookie Mix and stir until the mixture is well blended. Drop by rounded tablespoonfuls onto greased cookie sheet. Bake for 10 to 12 minutes. Transfer to wire racks to cool.

Chocolate Pecan Chewies Cookies
Makes 3 to 4 dozen cookies

1 jar Chocolate Pecan Chewies
  Cookie Mix
1/2 C. butter or margarine,
  softened

2 eggs, slightly beaten
1 tsp. vanilla

Preheat the oven to 375°F. In a large bowl, cream the butter, eggs and vanilla. Add the Chocolate Pecan Chewies Cookie Mix and stir until the mixture is well blended. Drop by rounded tablespoonfuls onto greased cookie sheet. Bake for 10 to 12 minutes. Transfer to wire racks to cool.

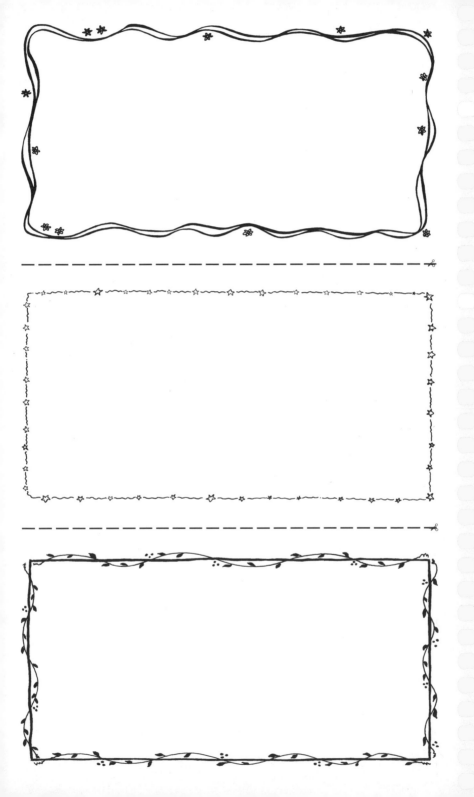

Vanilla & Chocolate Chip Cookie Mix

1/3 C. milk chocolate chips
1/3 C. vanilla chips
3/4 C. semi-sweet
   chocolate chips
2 C. all-purpose flour
1 tsp. baking soda
1 tsp. baking powder
1 C. sugar

Layer the ingredients in the order given into a wide-mouth 1-quart canning jar. Pack each layer in place before adding the next ingredient.

Attach a gift tag with the mixing and baking directions.

❀ *A half-yard of fabric should make eight wide-mouth jar covers.* ❀

Vanilla & Chocolate Chip Cookies

Makes 3 to 4 dozen cookies

1 jar Vanilla & Chocolate Chip
Cookie Mix
3/4 C. butter or margarine,
softened
2 eggs, slightly beaten
1 tsp. vanilla

Preheat the oven to 350°F. In a large bowl, cream the butter, eggs and vanilla. Add the Vanilla & Chocolate Chip Cookie Mix and stir until the mixture is well blended. Drop by rounded tablespoonfuls onto greased cookie sheet. Bake for 15 to 18 minutes. Transfer to wire racks to cool.

Vanilla & Chocolate Chip Cookies

Makes 3 to 4 dozen cookies

1 jar Vanilla & Chocolate Chip
  Cookie Mix
3/4 C. butter or margarine,
  softened

2 eggs, slightly beaten
1 tsp. vanilla

Preheat the oven to 350°F. In a large bowl, cream the butter, eggs and vanilla. Add the Vanilla & Chocolate Chip Cookie Mix and stir until the mixture is well blended. Drop by rounded tablespoonfuls onto greased cookie sheet. Bake for 15 to 18 minutes. Transfer to wire racks to cool.

Vanilla & Chocolate Chip Cookies

Makes 3 to 4 dozen cookies

1 jar Vanilla & Chocolate Chip
  Cookie Mix
3/4 C. butter or margarine,
  softened

2 eggs, slightly beaten
1 tsp. vanilla

Preheat the oven to 350°F. In a large bowl, cream the butter, eggs and vanilla. Add the Vanilla & Chocolate Chip Cookie Mix and stir until the mixture is well blended. Drop by rounded tablespoonfuls onto greased cookie sheet. Bake for 15 to 18 minutes. Transfer to wire racks to cool.

Vanilla & Chocolate Chip Cookies

Makes 3 to 4 dozen cookies

1 jar Vanilla & Chocolate Chip
  Cookie Mix
3/4 C. butter or margarine,
  softened

2 eggs, slightly beaten
1 tsp. vanilla

Preheat the oven to 350°F. In a large bowl, cream the butter, eggs and vanilla. Add the Vanilla & Chocolate Chip Cookie Mix and stir until the mixture is well blended. Drop by rounded tablespoonfuls onto greased cookie sheet. Bake for 15 to 18 minutes. Transfer to wire racks to cool.

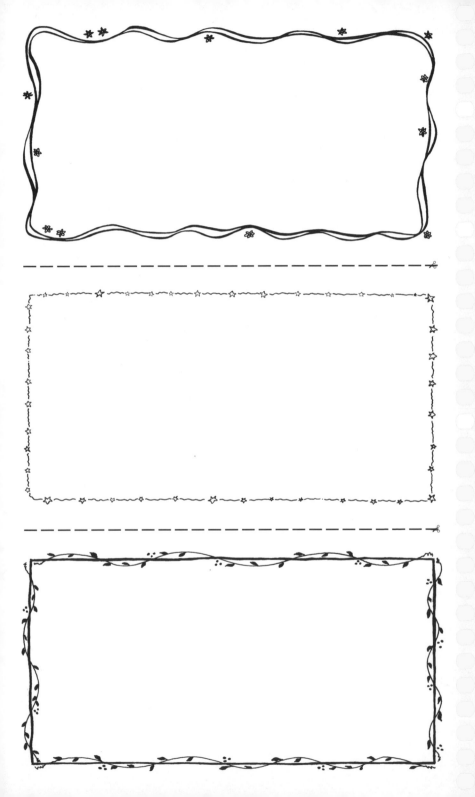

Vanilla & Chocolate Chip Cookies

Makes 3 to 4 dozen cookies

1 jar Vanilla & Chocolate Chip
  Cookie Mix
3/4 C. butter or margarine,
  softened

2 eggs, slightly beaten
1 tsp. vanilla

Preheat the oven to 350°F. In a large bowl, cream the butter, eggs and vanilla. Add the Vanilla & Chocolate Chip Cookie Mix and stir until the mixture is well blended. Drop by rounded tablespoonfuls onto greased cookie sheet. Bake for 15 to 18 minutes. Transfer to wire racks to cool.

Vanilla & Chocolate Chip Cookies

Makes 3 to 4 dozen cookies

1 jar Vanilla & Chocolate Chip
  Cookie Mix
3/4 C. butter or margarine,
  softened

2 eggs, slightly beaten
1 tsp. vanilla

Preheat the oven to 350°F. In a large bowl, cream the butter, eggs and vanilla. Add the Vanilla & Chocolate Chip Cookie Mix and stir until the mixture is well blended. Drop by rounded tablespoonfuls onto greased cookie sheet. Bake for 15 to 18 minutes. Transfer to wire racks to cool.

Vanilla & Chocolate Chip Cookies

Makes 3 to 4 dozen cookies

1 jar Vanilla & Chocolate Chip
  Cookie Mix
3/4 C. butter or margarine,
  softened

2 eggs, slightly beaten
1 tsp. vanilla

Preheat the oven to 350°F. In a large bowl, cream the butter, eggs and vanilla. Add the Vanilla & Chocolate Chip Cookie Mix and stir until the mixture is well blended. Drop by rounded tablespoonfuls onto greased cookie sheet. Bake for 15 to 18 minutes. Transfer to wire racks to cool.

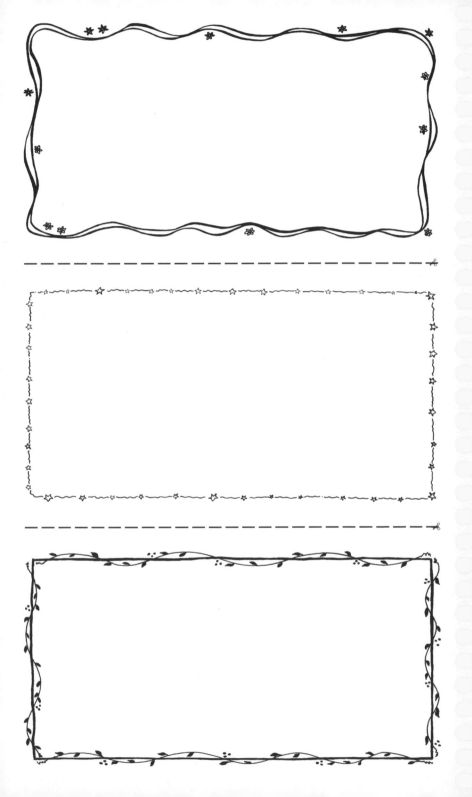

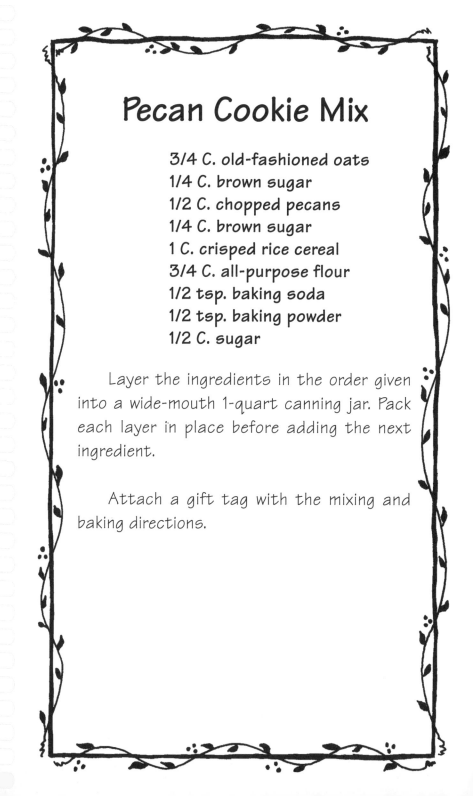

Pecan Cookie Mix

3/4 C. old-fashioned oats
1/4 C. brown sugar
1/2 C. chopped pecans
1/4 C. brown sugar
1 C. crisped rice cereal
3/4 C. all-purpose flour
1/2 tsp. baking soda
1/2 tsp. baking powder
1/2 C. sugar

Layer the ingredients in the order given into a wide-mouth 1-quart canning jar. Pack each layer in place before adding the next ingredient.

Attach a gift tag with the mixing and baking directions.

Pecan Cookies

Makes 3 to 4 dozen cookies

1 jar Pecan Cookie Mix
1/2 C. butter or margarine,
    softened
2 eggs, slightly beaten
1 tsp. vanilla

Preheat the oven to 350°F. In a large bowl, cream the butter, eggs and vanilla. Add the Pecan Cookie Mix and stir until the mixture is well blended. Drop by rounded tablespoonfuls onto greased cookie sheet. Bake for 10 to 12 minutes. Transfer to wire racks to cool.

Pecan Cookies
Makes 3 to 4 dozen cookies

1 jar Pecan Cookie Mix
1/2 C. butter or margarine,
  softened

2 eggs, slightly beaten
1 tsp. vanilla

Preheat the oven to 350°F. In a large bowl, cream the butter, eggs and vanilla. Add the Pecan Cookie Mix and stir until the mixture is well blended. Drop by rounded tablespoonfuls onto greased cookie sheet. Bake for 10 to 12 minutes. Transfer to wire racks to cool.

Pecan Cookies
Makes 3 to 4 dozen cookies

1 jar Pecan Cookie Mix
1/2 C. butter or margarine,
  softened

2 eggs, slightly beaten
1 tsp. vanilla

Preheat the oven to 350°F. In a large bowl, cream the butter, eggs and vanilla. Add the Pecan Cookie Mix and stir until the mixture is well blended. Drop by rounded tablespoonfuls onto greased cookie sheet. Bake for 10 to 12 minutes. Transfer to wire racks to cool.

Pecan Cookies
Makes 3 to 4 dozen cookies

1 jar Pecan Cookie Mix
1/2 C. butter or margarine,
  softened

2 eggs, slightly beaten
1 tsp. vanilla

Preheat the oven to 350°F. In a large bowl, cream the butter, eggs and vanilla. Add the Pecan Cookie Mix and stir until the mixture is well blended. Drop by rounded tablespoonfuls onto greased cookie sheet. Bake for 10 to 12 minutes. Transfer to wire racks to cool.

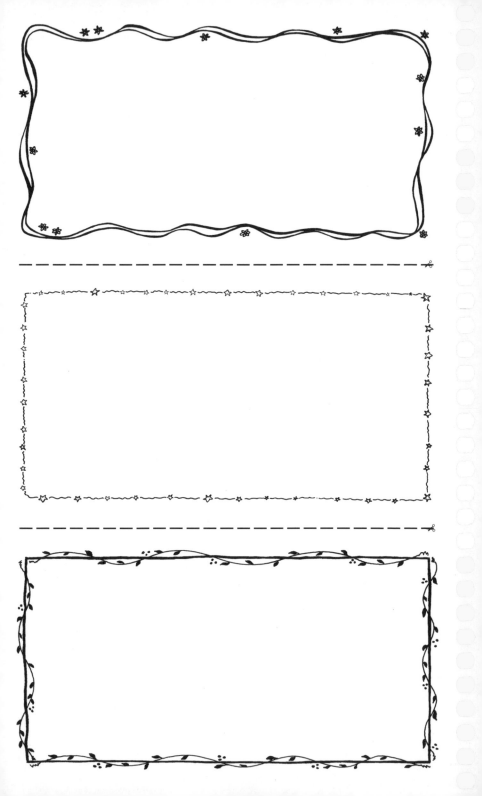

Pecan Cookies
Makes 3 to 4 dozen cookies

1 jar Pecan Cookie Mix
1/2 C. butter or margarine,
  softened

2 eggs, slightly beaten
1 tsp. vanilla

Preheat the oven to 350°F. In a large bowl, cream the butter, eggs and vanilla. Add the Pecan Cookie Mix and stir until the mixture is well blended. Drop by rounded tablespoonfuls onto greased cookie sheet. Bake for 10 to 12 minutes. Transfer to wire racks to cool.

Pecan Cookies
Makes 3 to 4 dozen cookies

1 jar Pecan Cookie Mix
1/2 C. butter or margarine,
  softened

2 eggs, slightly beaten
1 tsp. vanilla

Preheat the oven to 350°F. In a large bowl, cream the butter, eggs and vanilla. Add the Pecan Cookie Mix and stir until the mixture is well blended. Drop by rounded tablespoonfuls onto greased cookie sheet. Bake for 10 to 12 minutes. Transfer to wire racks to cool.

Pecan Cookies
Makes 3 to 4 dozen cookies

1 jar Pecan Cookie Mix
1/2 C. butter or margarine,
  softened

2 eggs, slightly beaten
1 tsp. vanilla

Preheat the oven to 350°F. In a large bowl, cream the butter, eggs and vanilla. Add the Pecan Cookie Mix and stir until the mixture is well blended. Drop by rounded tablespoonfuls onto greased cookie sheet. Bake for 10 to 12 minutes. Transfer to wire racks to cool.

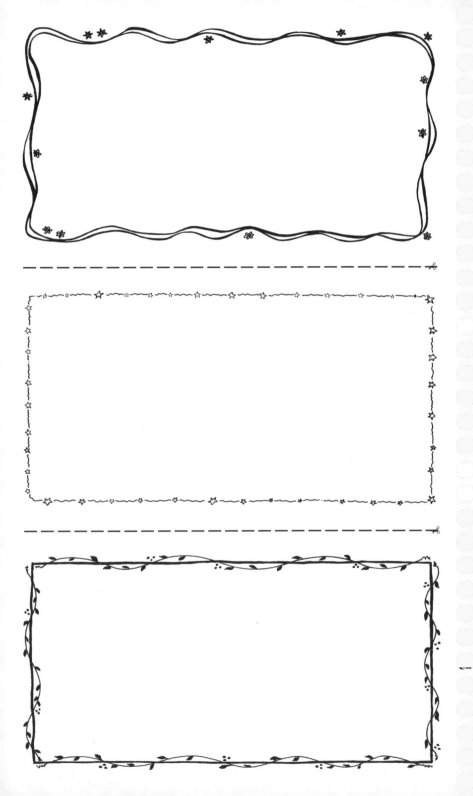

Molasses Cookie Mix

1 1/3 C. sugar
1 tsp. baking soda
1 tsp. baking powder
1 tsp. cinnamon
1/2 tsp. nutmeg
1/4 tsp. cloves
1/8 tsp. allspice
1 tsp. ginger
3 C. all-purpose flour

Layer the ingredients in the order given into a wide-mouth 1-quart canning jar. Pack each layer in place before adding the next ingredient.

Attach a gift tag with the mixing and baking directions.

Molasses Cookies

Makes 3 to 4 dozen cookies

1 jar Molasses Cookie Mix
1 C. butter or margarine,
  softened
2 eggs, slightly beaten
1/4 C. sweet molasses

Preheat the oven to 375°F. In a large bowl, cream the butter, eggs and molasses. Add the Molasses Cookie Mix and stir until the mixture is well blended. Drop by rounded tablespoonfuls onto greased cookie sheet. Bake for 10 to 12 minutes. Transfer to wire racks to cool.

Molasses Cookies
Makes 3 to 4 dozen cookies

1 jar Molasses Cookie Mix
1 C. butter or margarine,
softened

2 eggs, slightly beaten
1/4 C. sweet molasses

Preheat the oven to 375°F. In a large bowl, cream the butter, eggs and molasses. Add the Molasses Cookie Mix and stir until the mixture is well blended. Drop by rounded tablespoonfuls onto greased cookie sheet. Bake for 10 to 12 minutes. Transfer to wire racks to cool.

Molasses Cookies
Makes 3 to 4 dozen cookies

1 jar Molasses Cookie Mix
1 C. butter or margarine,
softened

2 eggs, slightly beaten
1/4 C. sweet molasses

Preheat the oven to 375°F. In a large bowl, cream the butter, eggs and molasses. Add the Molasses Cookie Mix and stir until the mixture is well blended. Drop by rounded tablespoonfuls onto greased cookie sheet. Bake for 10 to 12 minutes. Transfer to wire racks to cool.

Molasses Cookies
Makes 3 to 4 dozen cookies

1 jar Molasses Cookie Mix
1 C. butter or margarine,
softened

2 eggs, slightly beaten
1/4 C. sweet molasses

Preheat the oven to 375°F. In a large bowl, cream the butter, eggs and molasses. Add the Molasses Cookie Mix and stir until the mixture is well blended. Drop by rounded tablespoonfuls onto greased cookie sheet. Bake for 10 to 12 minutes. Transfer to wire racks to cool.

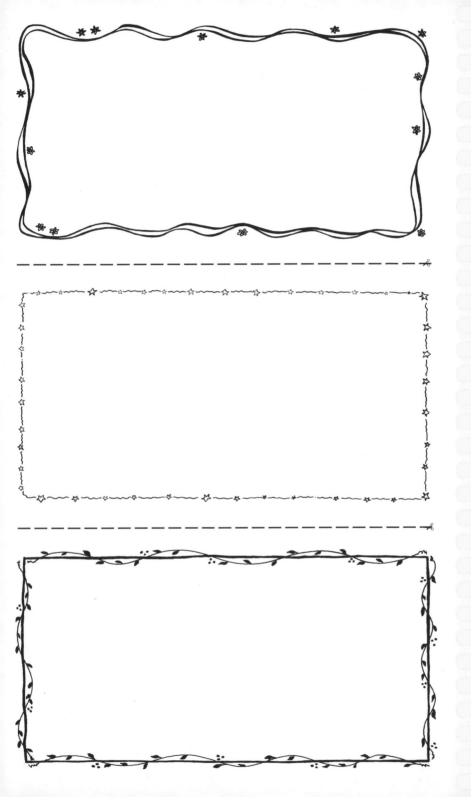

Molasses Cookies
Makes 3 to 4 dozen cookies

1 jar Molasses Cookie Mix
1 C. butter or margarine,
  softened

2 eggs, slightly beaten
1/4 C. sweet molasses

Preheat the oven to 375°F. In a large bowl, cream the butter, eggs and molasses. Add the Molasses Cookie Mix and stir until the mixture is well blended. Drop by rounded tablespoonfuls onto greased cookie sheet. Bake for 10 to 12 minutes. Transfer to wire racks to cool.

Molasses Cookies
Makes 3 to 4 dozen cookies

1 jar Molasses Cookie Mix
1 C. butter or margarine,
  softened

2 eggs, slightly beaten
1/4 C. sweet molasses

Preheat the oven to 375°F. In a large bowl, cream the butter, eggs and molasses. Add the Molasses Cookie Mix and stir until the mixture is well blended. Drop by rounded tablespoonfuls onto greased cookie sheet. Bake for 10 to 12 minutes. Transfer to wire racks to cool.

Molasses Cookies
Makes 3 to 4 dozen cookies

1 jar Molasses Cookie Mix
1 C. butter or margarine,
  softened

2 eggs, slightly beaten
1/4 C. sweet molasses

Preheat the oven to 375°F. In a large bowl, cream the butter, eggs and molasses. Add the Molasses Cookie Mix and stir until the mixture is well blended. Drop by rounded tablespoonfuls onto greased cookie sheet. Bake for 10 to 12 minutes. Transfer to wire racks to cool.

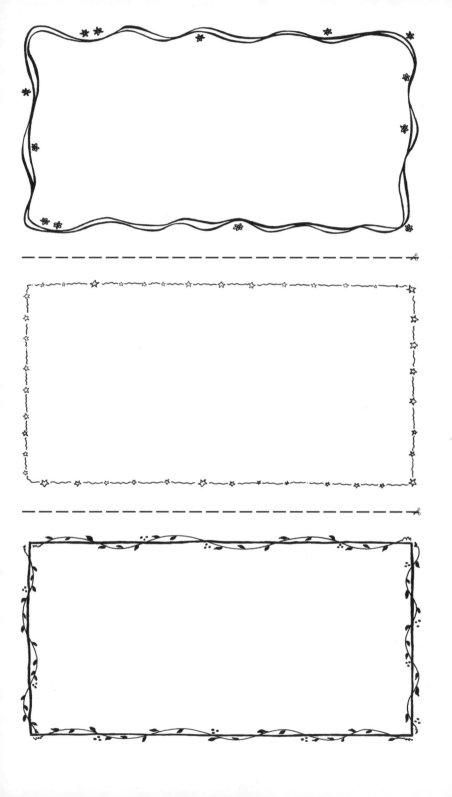

Candy Bar Cookie Mix

1/2 C. sugar
1/2 C. brown sugar
1 tsp. baking soda
2 C. all-purpose flour
1 C. your favorite candy bar,
    chopped

Layer the ingredients in the order given into a wide-mouth 1-quart canning jar. Pack each layer in place before adding the next ingredient.

Attach a gift tag with the mixing and baking directions.

Candy Bar Cookies

Makes 3 to 4 dozen cookies

1 jar Candy Bar Cookie Mix
3/4 C. butter or margarine,
   softened
2 eggs, slightly beaten
1 tsp. vanilla

Preheat the oven to 350°F. In a large bowl, cream the butter, eggs and vanilla. Add the Candy Bar Cookie Mix and stir until the mixture is well blended. Drop by rounded tablespoonfuls onto greased cookie sheet. Bake for 10 to 12 minutes. Transfer to wire racks to cool.

Candy Bar Cookies
Makes 3 to 4 dozen cookies

1 jar Candy Bar Cookie Mix
3/4 C. butter or margarine,
  softened

2 eggs, slightly beaten
1 tsp. vanilla

Preheat the oven to 350°F. In a large bowl, cream the butter, eggs and vanilla. Add the Candy Bar Cookie Mix and stir until the mixture is well blended. Drop by rounded tablespoonfuls onto greased cookie sheet. Bake for 10 to 12 minutes. Transfer to wire racks to cool.

Candy Bar Cookies
Makes 3 to 4 dozen cookies

1 jar Candy Bar Cookie Mix
3/4 C. butter or margarine,
  softened

2 eggs, slightly beaten
1 tsp. vanilla

Preheat the oven to 350°F. In a large bowl, cream the butter, eggs and vanilla. Add the Candy Bar Cookie Mix and stir until the mixture is well blended. Drop by rounded tablespoonfuls onto greased cookie sheet. Bake for 10 to 12 minutes. Transfer to wire racks to cool.

Candy Bar Cookies
Makes 3 to 4 dozen cookies

1 jar Candy Bar Cookie Mix
3/4 C. butter or margarine,
  softened

2 eggs, slightly beaten
1 tsp. vanilla

Preheat the oven to 350°F. In a large bowl, cream the butter, eggs and vanilla. Add the Candy Bar Cookie Mix and stir until the mixture is well blended. Drop by rounded tablespoonfuls onto greased cookie sheet. Bake for 10 to 12 minutes. Transfer to wire racks to cool.

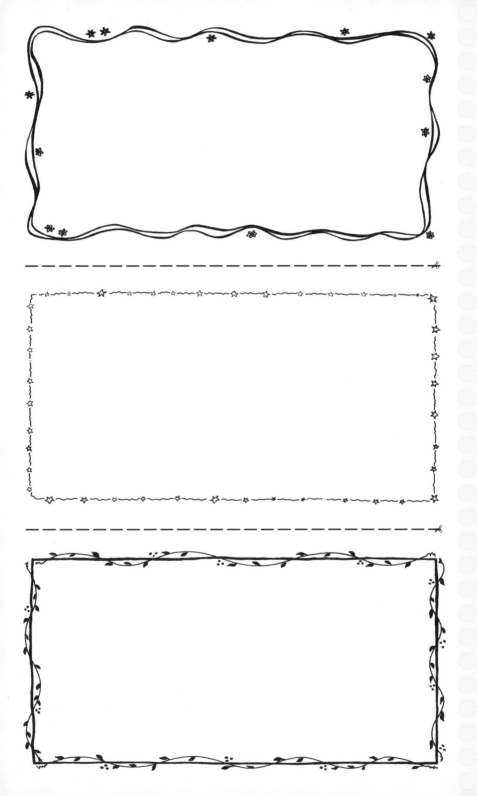

Candy Bar Cookies
Makes 3 to 4 dozen cookies

1 jar Candy Bar Cookie Mix
3/4 C. butter or margarine,
   softened

2 eggs, slightly beaten
1 tsp. vanilla

   Preheat the oven to 350°F. In a large bowl, cream the butter, eggs and vanilla. Add the Candy Bar Cookie Mix and stir until the mixture is well blended. Drop by rounded tablespoonfuls onto greased cookie sheet. Bake for 10 to 12 minutes. Transfer to wire racks to cool.

Candy Bar Cookies
Makes 3 to 4 dozen cookies

1 jar Candy Bar Cookie Mix
3/4 C. butter or margarine,
   softened

2 eggs, slightly beaten
1 tsp. vanilla

   Preheat the oven to 350°F. In a large bowl, cream the butter, eggs and vanilla. Add the Candy Bar Cookie Mix and stir until the mixture is well blended. Drop by rounded tablespoonfuls onto greased cookie sheet. Bake for 10 to 12 minutes. Transfer to wire racks to cool.

Candy Bar Cookies
Makes 3 to 4 dozen cookies

1 jar Candy Bar Cookie Mix
3/4 C. butter or margarine,
   softened

2 eggs, slightly beaten
1 tsp. vanilla

   Preheat the oven to 350°F. In a large bowl, cream the butter, eggs and vanilla. Add the Candy Bar Cookie Mix and stir until the mixture is well blended. Drop by rounded tablespoonfuls onto greased cookie sheet. Bake for 10 to 12 minutes. Transfer to wire racks to cool.

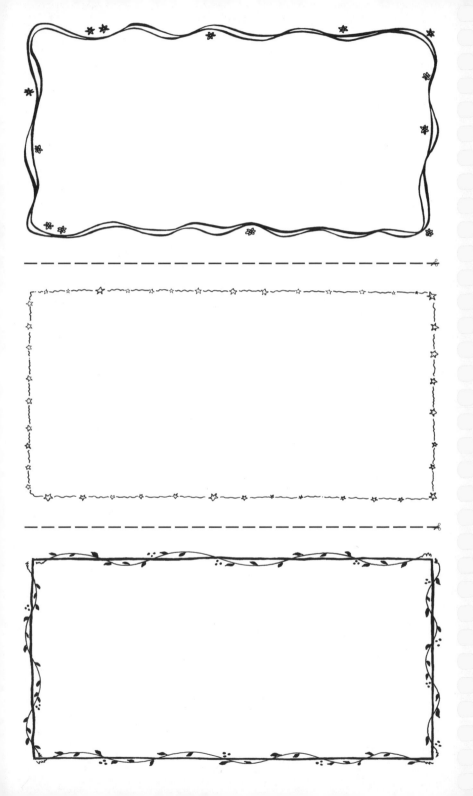

M&M Cookie Mix

1 C. M&M candies
2 C. all-purpose flour
1/2 tsp. baking soda
1/2 tsp. baking powder
1 1/4 C. sugar

Layer the ingredients in the order given into a wide-mouth 1-quart canning jar. Pack each layer in place before adding the next ingredient.

Attach a gift tag with the mixing and baking directions.

❀ *For a different look, place a small amount of stuffing under a fabric cover before attaching to "puff" the top.* ❀

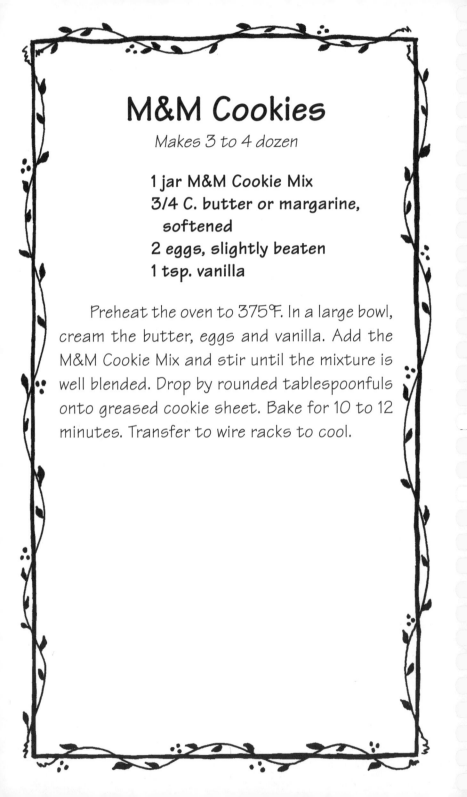

M&M Cookies

Makes 3 to 4 dozen

1 jar M&M Cookie Mix
3/4 C. butter or margarine,
  softened
2 eggs, slightly beaten
1 tsp. vanilla

Preheat the oven to 375°F. In a large bowl, cream the butter, eggs and vanilla. Add the M&M Cookie Mix and stir until the mixture is well blended. Drop by rounded tablespoonfuls onto greased cookie sheet. Bake for 10 to 12 minutes. Transfer to wire racks to cool.

M&M Cookies
Makes 3 to 4 dozen

1 jar M&M Cookie Mix
3/4 C. butter or margarine,
softened

2 eggs, slightly beaten
1 tsp. vanilla

Preheat the oven to 375°F. In a large bowl, cream the butter, eggs and vanilla. Add the M&M Cookie Mix and stir until the mixture is well blended. Drop by rounded tablespoonfuls onto greased cookie sheet. Bake for 10 to 12 minutes. Transfer to wire racks to cool.

M&M Cookies
Makes 3 to 4 dozen

1 jar M&M Cookie Mix
3/4 C. butter or margarine,
softened

2 eggs, slightly beaten
1 tsp. vanilla

Preheat the oven to 375°F. In a large bowl, cream the butter, eggs and vanilla. Add the M&M Cookie Mix and stir until the mixture is well blended. Drop by rounded tablespoonfuls onto greased cookie sheet. Bake for 10 to 12 minutes. Transfer to wire racks to cool.

M&M Cookies
Makes 3 to 4 dozen

1 jar M&M Cookie Mix
3/4 C. butter or margarine,
softened

2 eggs, slightly beaten
1 tsp. vanilla

Preheat the oven to 375°F. In a large bowl, cream the butter, eggs and vanilla. Add the M&M Cookie Mix and stir until the mixture is well blended. Drop by rounded tablespoonfuls onto greased cookie sheet. Bake for 10 to 12 minutes. Transfer to wire racks to cool.

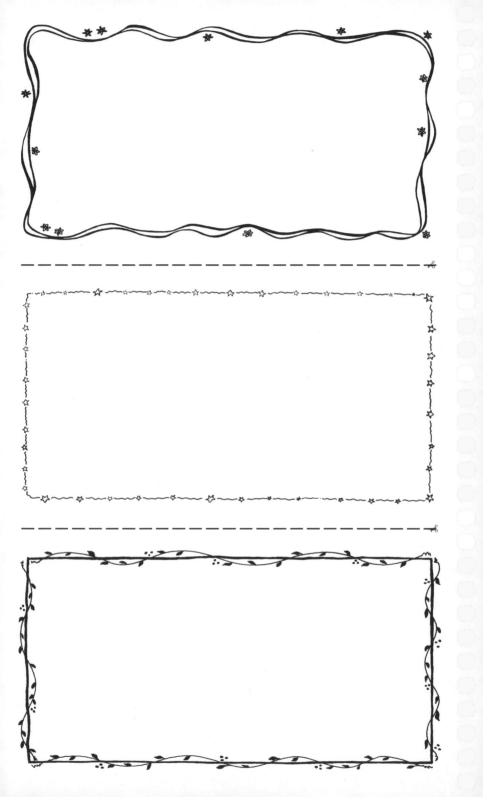

M&M Cookies
Makes 3 to 4 dozen

1 jar M&M Cookie Mix
3/4 C. butter or margarine,
softened

2 eggs, slightly beaten
1 tsp. vanilla

Preheat the oven to 375°F. In a large bowl, cream the butter, eggs and vanilla. Add the M&M Cookie Mix and stir until the mixture is well blended. Drop by rounded tablespoonfuls onto greased cookie sheet. Bake for 10 to 12 minutes. Transfer to wire racks to cool.

M&M Cookies
Makes 3 to 4 dozen

1 jar M&M Cookie Mix
3/4 C. butter or margarine,
softened

2 eggs, slightly beaten
1 tsp. vanilla

Preheat the oven to 375°F. In a large bowl, cream the butter, eggs and vanilla. Add the M&M Cookie Mix and stir until the mixture is well blended. Drop by rounded tablespoonfuls onto greased cookie sheet. Bake for 10 to 12 minutes. Transfer to wire racks to cool.

M&M Cookies
Makes 3 to 4 dozen

1 jar M&M Cookie Mix
3/4 C. butter or margarine,
softened

2 eggs, slightly beaten
1 tsp. vanilla

Preheat the oven to 375°F. In a large bowl, cream the butter, eggs and vanilla. Add the M&M Cookie Mix and stir until the mixture is well blended. Drop by rounded tablespoonfuls onto greased cookie sheet. Bake for 10 to 12 minutes. Transfer to wire racks to cool.

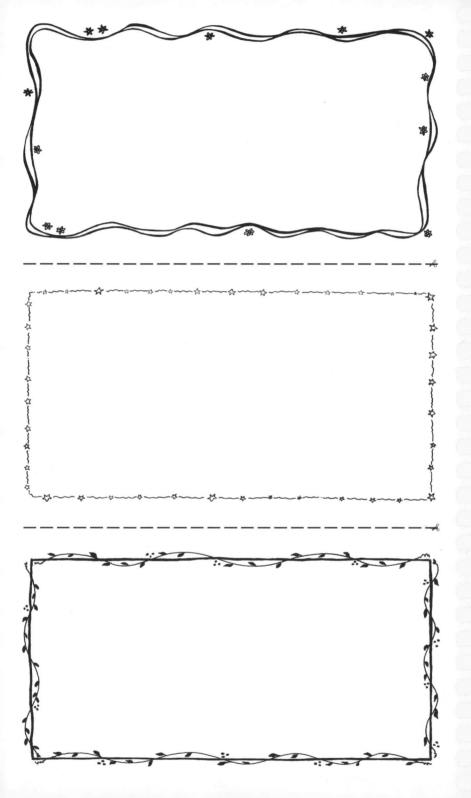

Oatmeal, Raisin & Spice Cookie Mix

1/2 C. raisins
1/2 C. sugar
1 tsp. ground cinnamon
1/2 tsp. ground nutmeg
1/2 C. brown sugar
2 C. all-purpose flour
1 tsp. baking soda
1/2 tsp. salt
1 C. old-fashioned oats

Layer the ingredients in the order given into a wide-mouth 1-quart canning jar. Pack each layer in place before adding the next ingredient.

Attach a gift tag with the mixing and baking directions.

Oatmeal, Raisin & Spice Cookies

Makes 3 to 4 dozen

1 jar Oatmeal, Raisin & Spice
   Cookie Mix
1/2 C. butter or margarine,
   softened
2 eggs, slightly beaten
1 tsp. vanilla

Preheat the oven to 375°F. In a large bowl, cream the butter, eggs and vanilla. Add the Oatmeal, Raisin & Spice Cookie Mix and stir until the mixture is well blended. Drop by rounded tablespoonfuls onto greased cookie sheet. Bake for 10 to 12 minutes. Transfer to wire racks to cool.

Oatmeal, Raisin & Spice Cookies

Makes 3 to 4 dozen

1 jar Oatmeal, Raisin & Spice
  Cookie Mix
1/2 C. butter or margarine,
  softened

2 eggs, slightly beaten
1 tsp. vanilla

Preheat the oven to 375°F. In a large bowl, cream the butter, eggs and vanilla. Add the Oatmeal, Raisin & Spice Cookie Mix and stir until the mixture is well blended. Drop by rounded tablespoonfuls onto greased cookie sheet. Bake for 10 to 12 minutes. Transfer to wire racks to cool.

Oatmeal, Raisin & Spice Cookies

Makes 3 to 4 dozen

1 jar Oatmeal, Raisin & Spice
  Cookie Mix
1/2 C. butter or margarine,
  softened

2 eggs, slightly beaten
1 tsp. vanilla

Preheat the oven to 375°F. In a large bowl, cream the butter, eggs and vanilla. Add the Oatmeal, Raisin & Spice Cookie Mix and stir until the mixture is well blended. Drop by rounded tablespoonfuls onto greased cookie sheet. Bake for 10 to 12 minutes. Transfer to wire racks to cool.

Oatmeal, Raisin & Spice Cookies

Makes 3 to 4 dozen

1 jar Oatmeal, Raisin & Spice
  Cookie Mix
1/2 C. butter or margarine,
  softened

2 eggs, slightly beaten
1 tsp. vanilla

Preheat the oven to 375°F. In a large bowl, cream the butter, eggs and vanilla. Add the Oatmeal, Raisin & Spice Cookie Mix and stir until the mixture is well blended. Drop by rounded tablespoonfuls onto greased cookie sheet. Bake for 10 to 12 minutes. Transfer to wire racks to cool.

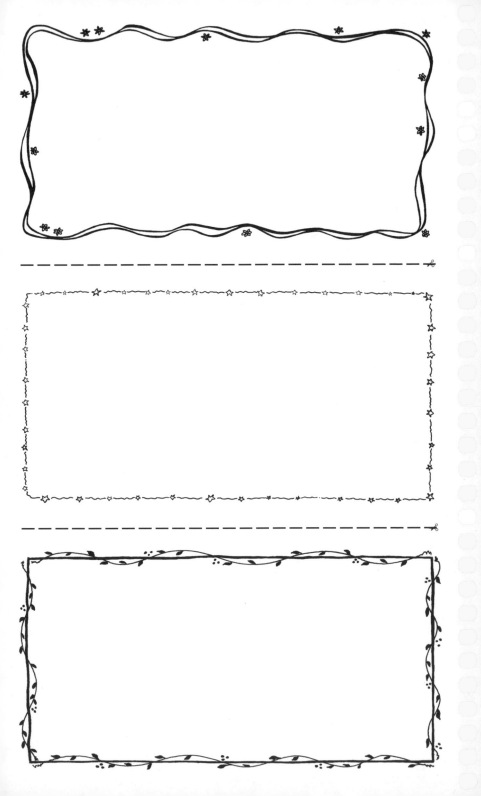

Oatmeal, Raisin & Spice Cookies
Makes 3 to 4 dozen

1 jar Oatmeal, Raisin & Spice
  Cookie Mix
1/2 C. butter or margarine,
  softened

2 eggs, slightly beaten
1 tsp. vanilla

    Preheat the oven to 375°F. In a large bowl, cream the butter, eggs and vanilla. Add the Oatmeal, Raisin & Spice Cookie Mix and stir until the mixture is well blended. Drop by rounded tablespoonfuls onto greased cookie sheet. Bake for 10 to 12 minutes. Transfer to wire racks to cool.

Oatmeal, Raisin & Spice Cookies
Makes 3 to 4 dozen

1 jar Oatmeal, Raisin & Spice
  Cookie Mix
1/2 C. butter or margarine,
  softened

2 eggs, slightly beaten
1 tsp. vanilla

    Preheat the oven to 375°F. In a large bowl, cream the butter, eggs and vanilla. Add the Oatmeal, Raisin & Spice Cookie Mix and stir until the mixture is well blended. Drop by rounded tablespoonfuls onto greased cookie sheet. Bake for 10 to 12 minutes. Transfer to wire racks to cool.

Oatmeal, Raisin & Spice Cookies
Makes 3 to 4 dozen

1 jar Oatmeal, Raisin & Spice
  Cookie Mix
1/2 C. butter or margarine,
  softened

2 eggs, slightly beaten
1 tsp. vanilla

    Preheat the oven to 375°F. In a large bowl, cream the butter, eggs and vanilla. Add the Oatmeal, Raisin & Spice Cookie Mix and stir until the mixture is well blended. Drop by rounded tablespoonfuls onto greased cookie sheet. Bake for 10 to 12 minutes. Transfer to wire racks to cool.

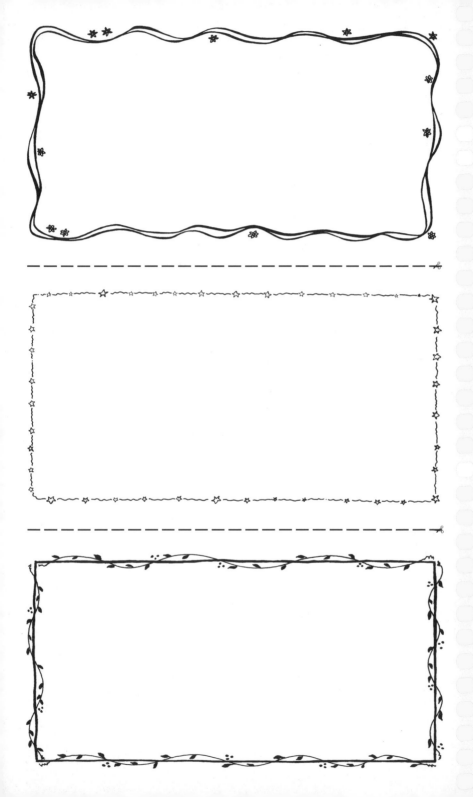

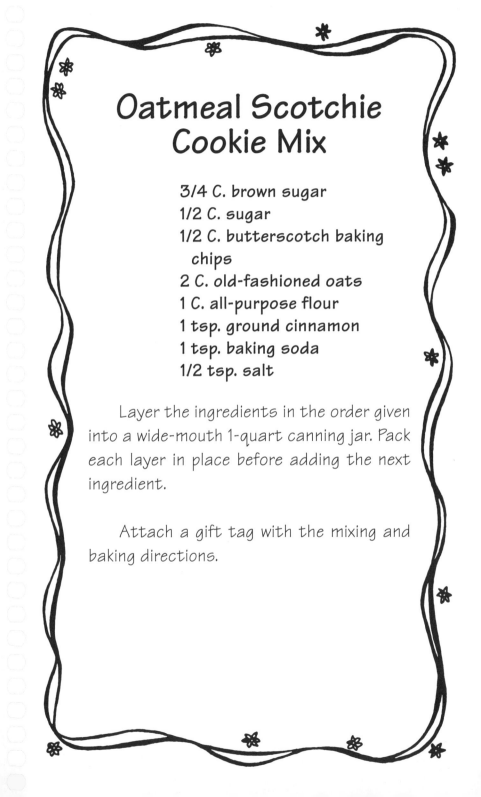

Oatmeal Scotchie Cookie Mix

3/4 C. brown sugar
1/2 C. sugar
1/2 C. butterscotch baking
   chips
2 C. old-fashioned oats
1 C. all-purpose flour
1 tsp. ground cinnamon
1 tsp. baking soda
1/2 tsp. salt

Layer the ingredients in the order given into a wide-mouth 1-quart canning jar. Pack each layer in place before adding the next ingredient.

Attach a gift tag with the mixing and baking directions.

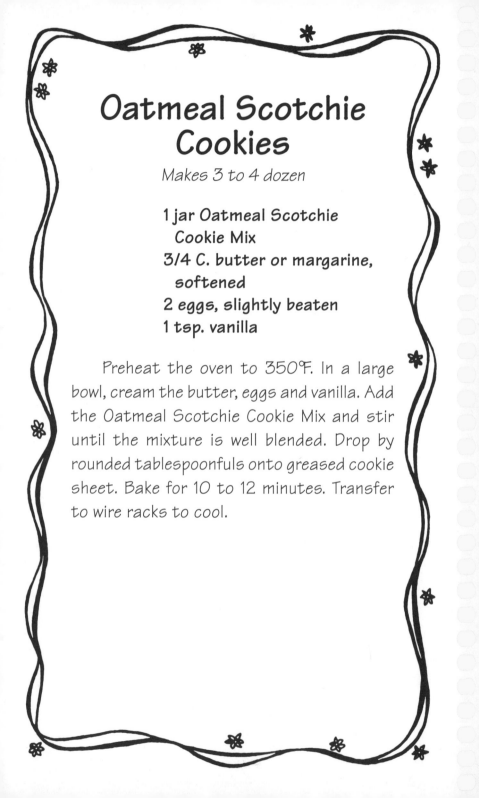

Oatmeal Scotchie Cookies

Makes 3 to 4 dozen

1 jar Oatmeal Scotchie
  Cookie Mix
3/4 C. butter or margarine,
  softened
2 eggs, slightly beaten
1 tsp. vanilla

Preheat the oven to 350°F. In a large bowl, cream the butter, eggs and vanilla. Add the Oatmeal Scotchie Cookie Mix and stir until the mixture is well blended. Drop by rounded tablespoonfuls onto greased cookie sheet. Bake for 10 to 12 minutes. Transfer to wire racks to cool.

Oatmeal Scotchie Cookies

Makes 3 to 4 dozen

1 jar Oatmeal Scotchie
  Cookie Mix
3/4 C. butter or margarine,
  softened

2 eggs, slightly beaten
1 tsp. vanilla

Preheat the oven to 350°F. In a large bowl, cream the butter, eggs and vanilla. Add the Oatmeal Scotchie Cookie Mix and stir until the mixture is well blended. Drop by rounded tablespoonfuls onto greased cookie sheet. Bake for 10 to 12 minutes. Transfer to wire racks to cool.

Oatmeal Scotchie Cookies

Makes 3 to 4 dozen

1 jar Oatmeal Scotchie
  Cookie Mix
3/4 C. butter or margarine,
  softened

2 eggs, slightly beaten
1 tsp. vanilla

Preheat the oven to 350°F. In a large bowl, cream the butter, eggs and vanilla. Add the Oatmeal Scotchie Cookie Mix and stir until the mixture is well blended. Drop by rounded tablespoonfuls onto greased cookie sheet. Bake for 10 to 12 minutes. Transfer to wire racks to cool.

Oatmeal Scotchie Cookies

Makes 3 to 4 dozen

1 jar Oatmeal Scotchie
  Cookie Mix
3/4 C. butter or margarine,
  softened

2 eggs, slightly beaten
1 tsp. vanilla

Preheat the oven to 350°F. In a large bowl, cream the butter, eggs and vanilla. Add the Oatmeal Scotchie Cookie Mix and stir until the mixture is well blended. Drop by rounded tablespoonfuls onto greased cookie sheet. Bake for 10 to 12 minutes. Transfer to wire racks to cool.

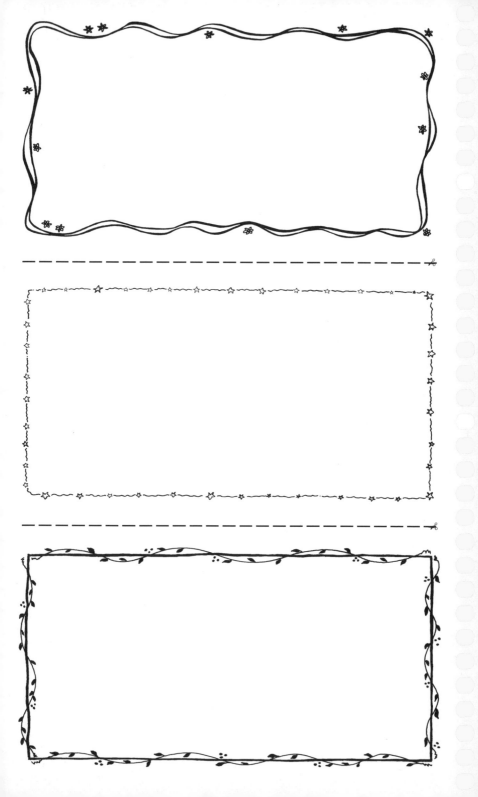

Oatmeal Scotchie Cookies
Makes 3 to 4 dozen

1 jar Oatmeal Scotchie
  Cookie Mix
3/4 C. butter or margarine,
  softened

2 eggs, slightly beaten
1 tsp. vanilla

Preheat the oven to 350°F. In a large bowl, cream the butter, eggs and vanilla. Add the Oatmeal Scotchie Cookie Mix and stir until the mixture is well blended. Drop by rounded tablespoonfuls onto greased cookie sheet. Bake for 10 to 12 minutes. Transfer to wire racks to cool.

Oatmeal Scotchie Cookies
Makes 3 to 4 dozen

1 jar Oatmeal Scotchie
  Cookie Mix
3/4 C. butter or margarine,
  softened

2 eggs, slightly beaten
1 tsp. vanilla

Preheat the oven to 350°F. In a large bowl, cream the butter, eggs and vanilla. Add the Oatmeal Scotchie Cookie Mix and stir until the mixture is well blended. Drop by rounded tablespoonfuls onto greased cookie sheet. Bake for 10 to 12 minutes. Transfer to wire racks to cool.

Oatmeal Scotchie Cookies
Makes 3 to 4 dozen

1 jar Oatmeal Scotchie
  Cookie Mix
3/4 C. butter or margarine,
  softened

2 eggs, slightly beaten
1 tsp. vanilla

Preheat the oven to 350°F. In a large bowl, cream the butter, eggs and vanilla. Add the Oatmeal Scotchie Cookie Mix and stir until the mixture is well blended. Drop by rounded tablespoonfuls onto greased cookie sheet. Bake for 10 to 12 minutes. Transfer to wire racks to cool.

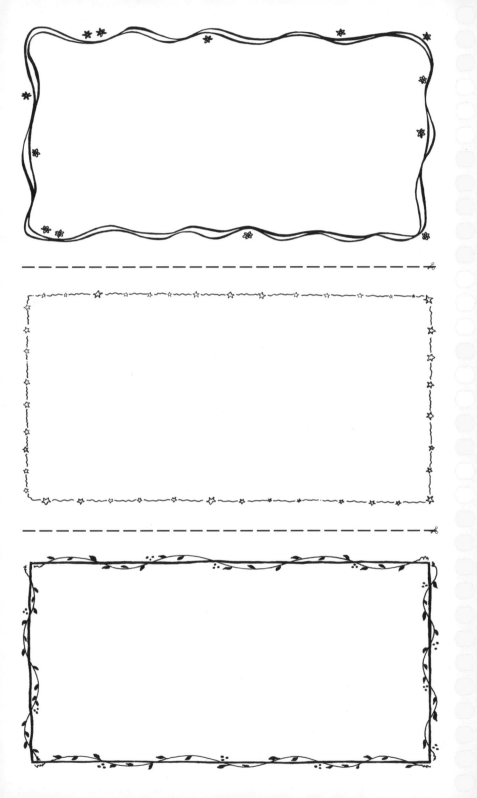

White Chocolate-Macadamia Nut Cookie Mix

1 1/4 C. sugar
1/2 C. chopped macadamia nuts
1 C. white chocolate baking chips
2 C. all-purpose flour
1/2 tsp. baking soda
1/2 tsp. baking powder

Layer the ingredients in the order given into a wide-mouth 1-quart canning jar. Pack each layer in place before adding the next ingredient.

Attach a gift tag with the mixing and baking directions.

❀ *Wrap a cookie mix in a decorative towel and place it into a new cookie jar for an extra special gift.* ❀

White Chocolate-Macadamia Nut Cookies

Makes 3 to 4 dozen

1 jar White Chocolate-
   Macadamia Nut Cookie Mix
1 C. butter or margarine,
   softened
2 eggs, slightly beaten
2 tsp. vanilla

Preheat the oven to 375°F. In a large bowl, cream the butter, eggs and vanilla. Add the White Chocolate-Macadamia Nut Cookie Mix and stir until the mixture is well blended. Drop by rounded tablespoonfuls onto greased cookie sheet. Bake for 12 to 14 minutes. Transfer to wire racks to cool.

White Chocolate-Macadamia Nut Cookies
Makes 3 to 4 dozen

1 jar White Chocolate-
 Macadamia Nut Cookie Mix
1 C. butter or margarine,
 softened

2 eggs, slightly beaten
2 tsp. vanilla

Preheat the oven to 375°F. In a large bowl, cream the butter, eggs and vanilla. Add the White Chocolate-Macadamia Nut Cookie Mix and stir until the mixture is well blended. Drop by rounded tablespoonfuls onto greased cookie sheet. Bake for 12 to 14 minutes. Transfer to wire racks to cool.

White Chocolate-Macadamia Nut Cookies
Makes 3 to 4 dozen

1 jar White Chocolate-
 Macadamia Nut Cookie Mix
1 C. butter or margarine,
 softened

2 eggs, slightly beaten
2 tsp. vanilla

Preheat the oven to 375°F. In a large bowl, cream the butter, eggs and vanilla. Add the White Chocolate-Macadamia Nut Cookie Mix and stir until the mixture is well blended. Drop by rounded tablespoonfuls onto greased cookie sheet. Bake for 12 to 14 minutes. Transfer to wire racks to cool.

White Chocolate-Macadamia Nut Cookies
Makes 3 to 4 dozen

1 jar White Chocolate-
 Macadamia Nut Cookie Mix
1 C. butter or margarine,
 softened

2 eggs, slightly beaten
2 tsp. vanilla

Preheat the oven to 375°F. In a large bowl, cream the butter, eggs and vanilla. Add the White Chocolate-Macadamia Nut Cookie Mix and stir until the mixture is well blended. Drop by rounded tablespoonfuls onto greased cookie sheet. Bake for 12 to 14 minutes. Transfer to wire racks to cool.

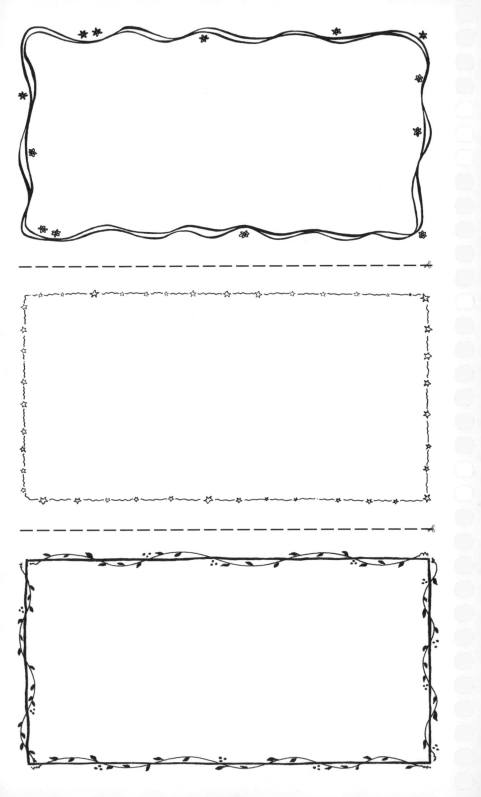

White Chocolate-Macadamia Nut Cookies
Makes 3 to 4 dozen

1 jar White Chocolate-
    Macadamia Nut Cookie Mix
1 C. butter or margarine,
    softened

2 eggs, slightly beaten
2 tsp. vanilla

Preheat the oven to 375°F. In a large bowl, cream the butter, eggs and vanilla. Add the White Chocolate-Macadamia Nut Cookie Mix and stir until the mixture is well blended. Drop by rounded tablespoonfuls onto greased cookie sheet. Bake for 12 to 14 minutes. Transfer to wire racks to cool.

White Chocolate-Macadamia Nut Cookies
Makes 3 to 4 dozen

1 jar White Chocolate-
    Macadamia Nut Cookie Mix
1 C. butter or margarine,
    softened

2 eggs, slightly beaten
2 tsp. vanilla

Preheat the oven to 375°F. In a large bowl, cream the butter, eggs and vanilla. Add the White Chocolate-Macadamia Nut Cookie Mix and stir until the mixture is well blended. Drop by rounded tablespoonfuls onto greased cookie sheet. Bake for 12 to 14 minutes. Transfer to wire racks to cool.

White Chocolate-Macadamia Nut Cookies
Makes 3 to 4 dozen

1 jar White Chocolate-
    Macadamia Nut Cookie Mix
1 C. butter or margarine,
    softened

2 eggs, slightly beaten
2 tsp. vanilla

Preheat the oven to 375°F. In a large bowl, cream the butter, eggs and vanilla. Add the White Chocolate-Macadamia Nut Cookie Mix and stir until the mixture is well blended. Drop by rounded tablespoonfuls onto greased cookie sheet. Bake for 12 to 14 minutes. Transfer to wire racks to cool.

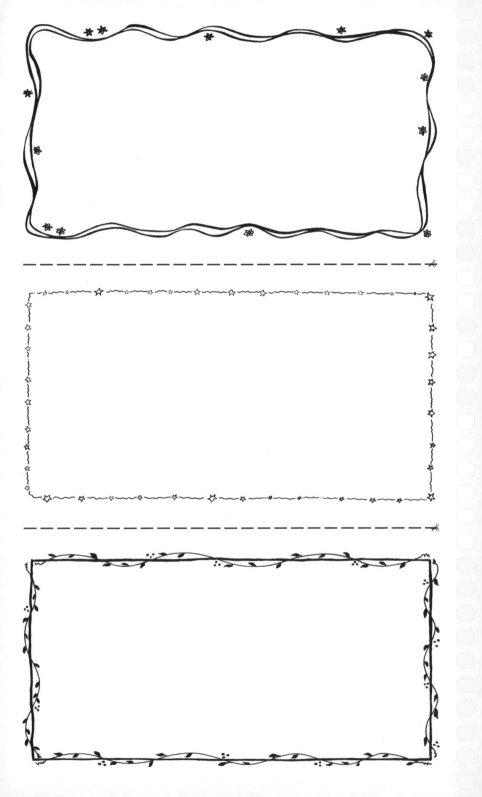

Chunky Chocolate Cookie Mix

3/4 C. brown sugar
1/2 C. sugar
1/4 C. cocoa powder (clean
   inside of jar with a paper
   towel after this layer)
1/2 C. chopped pecans
1 C. jumbo chocolate chips
1 3/4 C. all-purpose flour
1 tsp. baking soda
1 tsp. baking powder
1/4 tsp. salt

Layer the ingredients in the order given into a wide-mouth 1-quart canning jar. Pack each layer in place before adding the next ingredient.

Attach a gift tag with the mixing and baking directions.

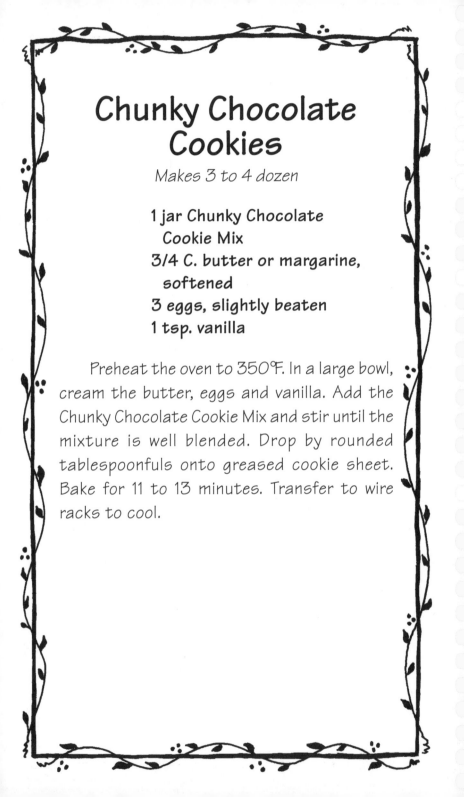

Chunky Chocolate Cookies

Makes 3 to 4 dozen

1 jar Chunky Chocolate
   Cookie Mix
3/4 C. butter or margarine,
   softened
3 eggs, slightly beaten
1 tsp. vanilla

Preheat the oven to 350°F. In a large bowl, cream the butter, eggs and vanilla. Add the Chunky Chocolate Cookie Mix and stir until the mixture is well blended. Drop by rounded tablespoonfuls onto greased cookie sheet. Bake for 11 to 13 minutes. Transfer to wire racks to cool.

Chunky Chocolate Cookies
Makes 3 to 4 dozen

1 jar Chunky Chocolate
    Cookie Mix
3/4 C. butter or margarine,
    softened

3 eggs, slightly beaten
1 tsp. vanilla

Preheat the oven to 350°F. In a large bowl, cream the butter, eggs and vanilla. Add the Chunky Chocolate Cookie Mix and stir until the mixture is well blended. Drop by rounded tablespoonfuls onto greased cookie sheet. Bake for 11 to 13 minutes. Transfer to wire racks to cool.

Chunky Chocolate Cookies
Makes 3 to 4 dozen

1 jar Chunky Chocolate
    Cookie Mix
3/4 C. butter or margarine,
    softened

3 eggs, slightly beaten
1 tsp. vanilla

Preheat the oven to 350°F. In a large bowl, cream the butter, eggs and vanilla. Add the Chunky Chocolate Cookie Mix and stir until the mixture is well blended. Drop by rounded tablespoonfuls onto greased cookie sheet. Bake for 11 to 13 minutes. Transfer to wire racks to cool.

Chunky Chocolate Cookies
Makes 3 to 4 dozen

1 jar Chunky Chocolate
    Cookie Mix
3/4 C. butter or margarine,
    softened

3 eggs, slightly beaten
1 tsp. vanilla

Preheat the oven to 350°F. In a large bowl, cream the butter, eggs and vanilla. Add the Chunky Chocolate Cookie Mix and stir until the mixture is well blended. Drop by rounded tablespoonfuls onto greased cookie sheet. Bake for 11 to 13 minutes. Transfer to wire racks to cool.

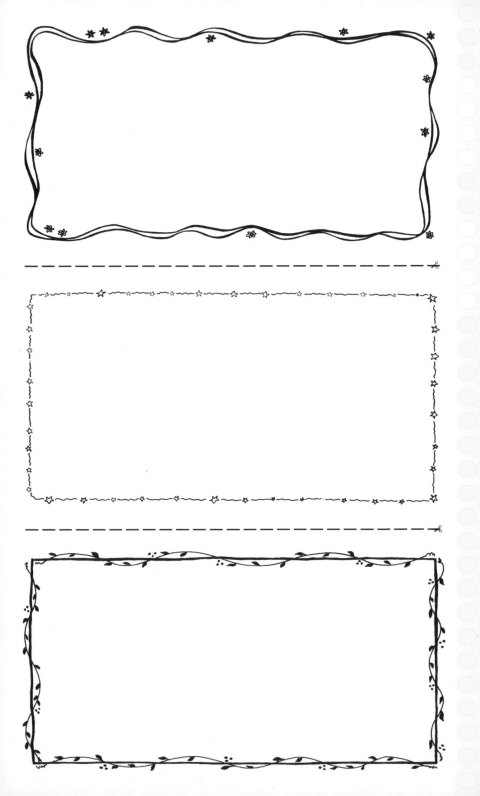

Chunky Chocolate Cookies
Makes 3 to 4 dozen

1 jar Chunky Chocolate
   Cookie Mix
3/4 C. butter or margarine,
   softened

3 eggs, slightly beaten
1 tsp. vanilla

   Preheat the oven to 350°F. In a large bowl, cream the butter, eggs and vanilla. Add the Chunky Chocolate Cookie Mix and stir until the mixture is well blended. Drop by rounded tablespoonfuls onto greased cookie sheet. Bake for 11 to 13 minutes. Transfer to wire racks to cool.

Chunky Chocolate Cookies
Makes 3 to 4 dozen

1 jar Chunky Chocolate
   Cookie Mix
3/4 C. butter or margarine,
   softened

3 eggs, slightly beaten
1 tsp. vanilla

   Preheat the oven to 350°F. In a large bowl, cream the butter, eggs and vanilla. Add the Chunky Chocolate Cookie Mix and stir until the mixture is well blended. Drop by rounded tablespoonfuls onto greased cookie sheet. Bake for 11 to 13 minutes. Transfer to wire racks to cool.

Chunky Chocolate Cookies
Makes 3 to 4 dozen

1 jar Chunky Chocolate
   Cookie Mix
3/4 C. butter or margarine,
   softened

3 eggs, slightly beaten
1 tsp. vanilla

   Preheat the oven to 350°F. In a large bowl, cream the butter, eggs and vanilla. Add the Chunky Chocolate Cookie Mix and stir until the mixture is well blended. Drop by rounded tablespoonfuls onto greased cookie sheet. Bake for 11 to 13 minutes. Transfer to wire racks to cool.

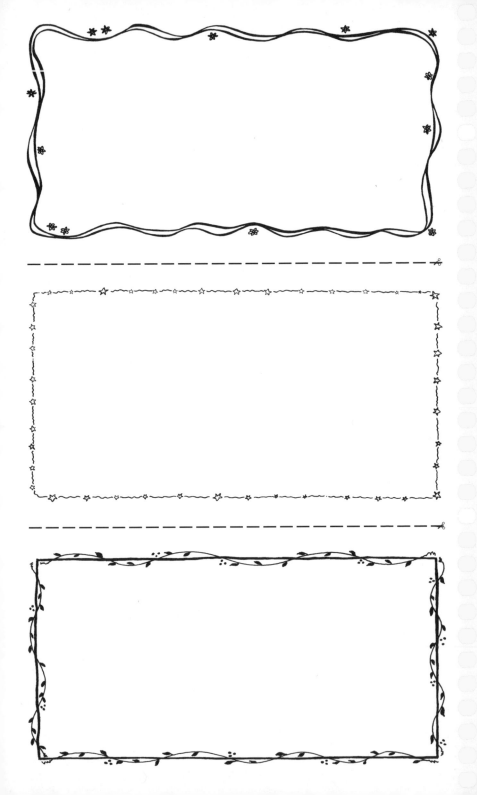

Peanut Butter Chocolate Chip Cookie Mix

3/4 C. sugar
3/4 C. brown sugar
1 C. chocolate chips
2 C. all-purpose flour
1/2 tsp. baking soda
1/4 tsp. salt

Layer the ingredients in the order given into a wide-mouth 1-quart canning jar. Pack each layer in place before adding the next ingredient.

Attach a gift tag with the mixing and baking directions.

Peanut Butter Chocolate Chip Cookies

Makes 3 to 4 dozen

1 jar Peanut Butter Chocolate
    Chip Cookie Mix
1 C. butter or margarine,
    softened
2 eggs, slightly beaten
2 tsp. vanilla
1 C. creamy peanut butter

Preheat the oven to 350°F. In a large bowl, cream the butter, eggs and vanilla. Blend in the peanut butter. Add the Peanut Butter Chocolate Chip Cookie Mix and stir until the mixture is well blended. Drop by rounded tablespoonfuls onto greased cookie sheet. Bake for 9 to 11 minutes. Transfer to wire racks to cool.

Peanut Butter Chocolate Chip Cookies
Makes 3 to 4 dozen

1 jar Peanut Butter Chocolate
   Chip Cookie Mix
1 C. butter or margarine,
   softened

2 eggs, slightly beaten
2 tsp. vanilla
1 C. creamy peanut butter

Preheat the oven to 350°F. In a large bowl, cream the butter, eggs and vanilla. Blend in the peanut butter. Add the Peanut Butter Chocolate Chip Cookie Mix and stir until the mixture is well blended. Drop by rounded tablespoonfuls onto greased cookie sheet. Bake for 9 to 11 minutes. Transfer to wire racks to cool.

Peanut Butter Chocolate Chip Cookies
Makes 3 to 4 dozen

1 jar Peanut Butter Chocolate
   Chip Cookie Mix
1 C. butter or margarine,
   softened

2 eggs, slightly beaten
2 tsp. vanilla
1 C. creamy peanut butter

Preheat the oven to 350°F. In a large bowl, cream the butter, eggs and vanilla. Blend in the peanut butter. Add the Peanut Butter Chocolate Chip Cookie Mix and stir until the mixture is well blended. Drop by rounded tablespoonfuls onto greased cookie sheet. Bake for 9 to 11 minutes. Transfer to wire racks to cool.

Peanut Butter Chocolate Chip Cookies
Makes 3 to 4 dozen

1 jar Peanut Butter Chocolate
   Chip Cookie Mix
1 C. butter or margarine,
   softened

2 eggs, slightly beaten
2 tsp. vanilla
1 C. creamy peanut butter

Preheat the oven to 350°F. In a large bowl, cream the butter, eggs and vanilla. Blend in the peanut butter. Add the Peanut Butter Chocolate Chip Cookie Mix and stir until the mixture is well blended. Drop by rounded tablespoonfuls onto greased cookie sheet. Bake for 9 to 11 minutes. Transfer to wire racks to cool.

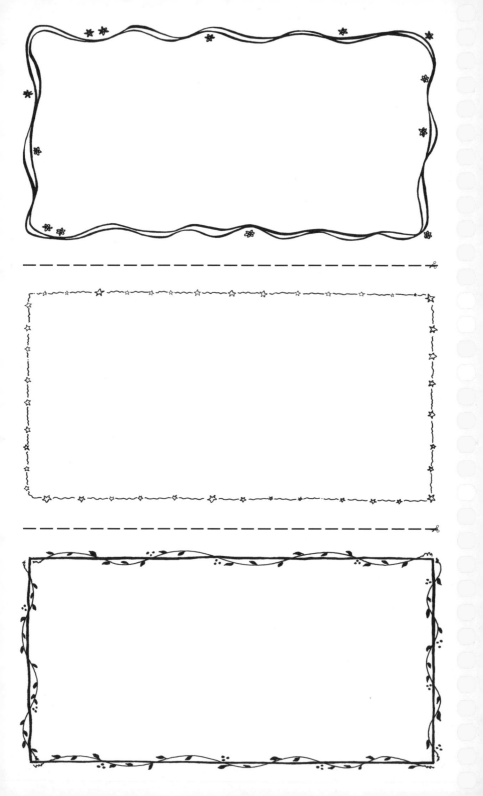

Peanut Butter Chocolate Chip Cookies
Makes 3 to 4 dozen

1 jar Peanut Butter Chocolate
  Chip Cookie Mix
1 C. butter or margarine,
  softened

2 eggs, slightly beaten
2 tsp. vanilla
1 C. creamy peanut butter

Preheat the oven to 350°F. In a large bowl, cream the butter, eggs and vanilla. Blend in the peanut butter. Add the Peanut Butter Chocolate Chip Cookie Mix and stir until the mixture is well blended. Drop by rounded tablespoonfuls onto greased cookie sheet. Bake for 9 to 11 minutes. Transfer to wire racks to cool.

Peanut Butter Chocolate Chip Cookies
Makes 3 to 4 dozen

1 jar Peanut Butter Chocolate
  Chip Cookie Mix
1 C. butter or margarine,
  softened

2 eggs, slightly beaten
2 tsp. vanilla
1 C. creamy peanut butter

Preheat the oven to 350°F. In a large bowl, cream the butter, eggs and vanilla. Blend in the peanut butter. Add the Peanut Butter Chocolate Chip Cookie Mix and stir until the mixture is well blended. Drop by rounded tablespoonfuls onto greased cookie sheet. Bake for 9 to 11 minutes. Transfer to wire racks to cool.

Peanut Butter Chocolate Chip Cookies
Makes 3 to 4 dozen

1 jar Peanut Butter Chocolate
  Chip Cookie Mix
1 C. butter or margarine,
  softened

2 eggs, slightly beaten
2 tsp. vanilla
1 C. creamy peanut butter

Preheat the oven to 350°F. In a large bowl, cream the butter, eggs and vanilla. Blend in the peanut butter. Add the Peanut Butter Chocolate Chip Cookie Mix and stir until the mixture is well blended. Drop by rounded tablespoonfuls onto greased cookie sheet. Bake for 9 to 11 minutes. Transfer to wire racks to cool.

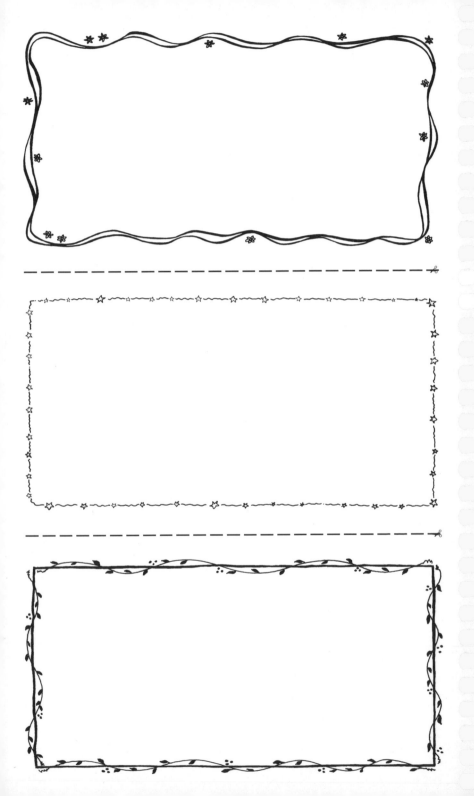

Trail Cookie Mix

1/2 C. brown sugar
1/2 C. sugar
3/4 C. wheat germ
1/3 C. quick oats
1 C. raisins
1/3 C. flaked coconut
1/2 C. chopped pecans
3/4 C. all-purpose flour
1 tsp. baking powder

Layer the ingredients in the order given into a wide-mouth 1-quart canning jar. Pack each layer in place before adding the next ingredient.

Attach a gift tag with the mixing and baking directions.

❀ *To make a gift in a jar fancier, decorate it with a doily and ribbon.* ❀

Trail Cookies

Makes 3 to 4 dozen

1 jar Trail Cookie Mix
1/2 C. butter or margarine,
   softened
2 eggs, slightly beaten
1 tsp. vanilla

Preheat the oven to 350°F. In a large bowl, cream the butter, eggs and vanilla. Add the Trail Cookie Mix and stir until the mixture is well blended. Drop by rounded tablespoonfuls onto greased cookie sheet. Bake for 12 to 14 minutes. Transfer to wire racks to cool.

Trail Cookies
Makes 3 to 4 dozen

1 jar Trail Cookie Mix
1/2 C. butter or margarine,
   softened

2 eggs, slightly beaten
1 tsp. vanilla

Preheat the oven to 350°F. In a large bowl, cream the butter, eggs and vanilla. Add the Trail Cookie Mix and stir until the mixture is well blended. Drop by rounded tablespoonfuls onto greased cookie sheet. Bake for 12 to 14 minutes. Transfer to wire racks to cool.

Trail Cookies
Makes 3 to 4 dozen

1 jar Trail Cookie Mix
1/2 C. butter or margarine,
   softened

2 eggs, slightly beaten
1 tsp. vanilla

Preheat the oven to 350°F. In a large bowl, cream the butter, eggs and vanilla. Add the Trail Cookie Mix and stir until the mixture is well blended. Drop by rounded tablespoonfuls onto greased cookie sheet. Bake for 12 to 14 minutes. Transfer to wire racks to cool.

Trail Cookies
Makes 3 to 4 dozen

1 jar Trail Cookie Mix
1/2 C. butter or margarine,
   softened

2 eggs, slightly beaten
1 tsp. vanilla

Preheat the oven to 350°F. In a large bowl, cream the butter, eggs and vanilla. Add the Trail Cookie Mix and stir until the mixture is well blended. Drop by rounded tablespoonfuls onto greased cookie sheet. Bake for 12 to 14 minutes. Transfer to wire racks to cool.

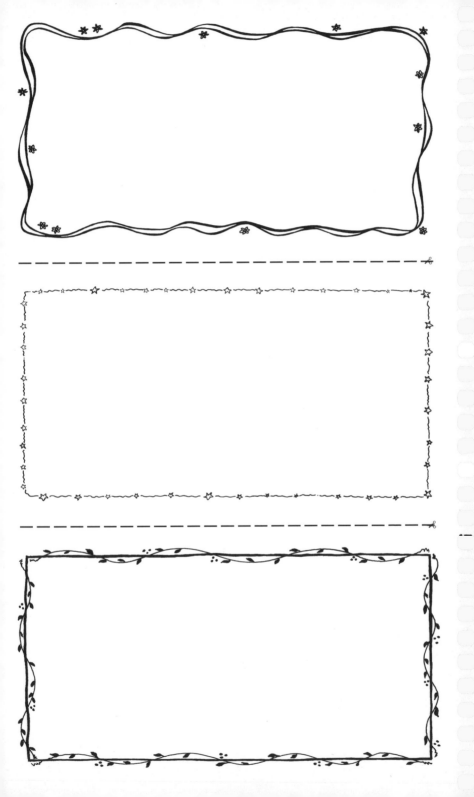

Trail Cookies
Makes 3 to 4 dozen

1 jar Trail Cookie Mix
1/2 C. butter or margarine,
   softened

2 eggs, slightly beaten
1 tsp. vanilla

Preheat the oven to 350°F. In a large bowl, cream the butter, eggs and vanilla. Add the Trail Cookie Mix and stir until the mixture is well blended. Drop by rounded tablespoonfuls onto greased cookie sheet. Bake for 12 to 14 minutes. Transfer to wire racks to cool.

Trail Cookies
Makes 3 to 4 dozen

1 jar Trail Cookie Mix
1/2 C. butter or margarine,
   softened

2 eggs, slightly beaten
1 tsp. vanilla

Preheat the oven to 350°F. In a large bowl, cream the butter, eggs and vanilla. Add the Trail Cookie Mix and stir until the mixture is well blended. Drop by rounded tablespoonfuls onto greased cookie sheet. Bake for 12 to 14 minutes. Transfer to wire racks to cool.

Trail Cookies
Makes 3 to 4 dozen

1 jar Trail Cookie Mix
1/2 C. butter or margarine,
   softened

2 eggs, slightly beaten
1 tsp. vanilla

Preheat the oven to 350°F. In a large bowl, cream the butter, eggs and vanilla. Add the Trail Cookie Mix and stir until the mixture is well blended. Drop by rounded tablespoonfuls onto greased cookie sheet. Bake for 12 to 14 minutes. Transfer to wire racks to cool.

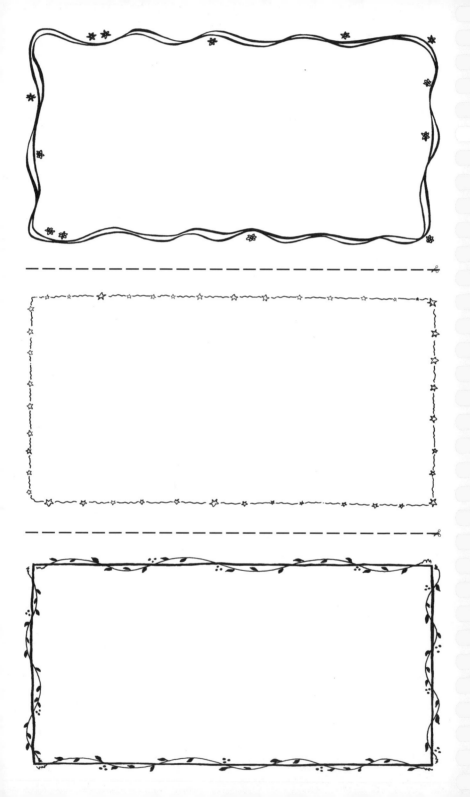

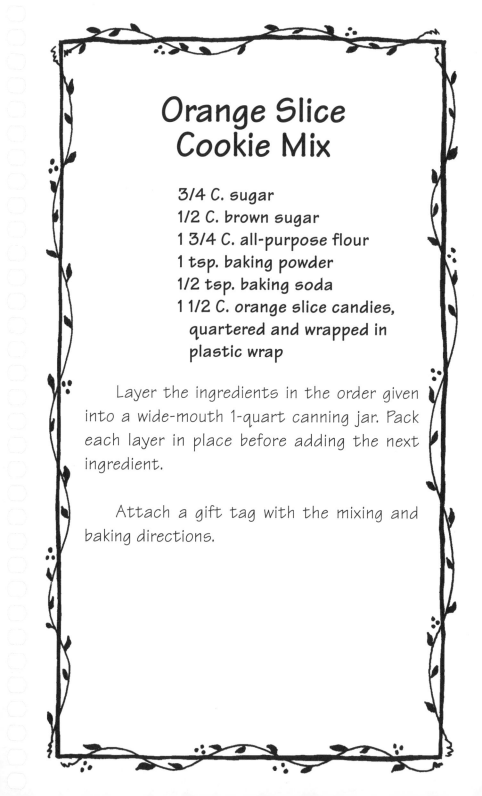

Orange Slice Cookie Mix

3/4 C. sugar
1/2 C. brown sugar
1 3/4 C. all-purpose flour
1 tsp. baking powder
1/2 tsp. baking soda
1 1/2 C. orange slice candies,
   quartered and wrapped in
   plastic wrap

Layer the ingredients in the order given into a wide-mouth 1-quart canning jar. Pack each layer in place before adding the next ingredient.

Attach a gift tag with the mixing and baking directions.

Orange Slice Cookies

Makes 3 to 4 dozen

1 jar Orange Slice Cookie Mix
1/2 C. butter or margarine,
   softened
2 eggs, slightly beaten
1 tsp. vanilla

Preheat the oven to 375°F. In a large bowl, cream the butter, eggs and vanilla. Remove the orange slice candies from the jar and set aside. Add the Orange Slice Cookie Mix and stir until the mixture is well blended. Stir in orange slice candies. Drop by rounded tablespoonfuls onto greased cookie sheet. Bake for 12 to 14 minutes. Transfer to wire racks to cool.

Orange Slice Cookies
Makes 3 to 4 dozen

1 jar Orange Slice Cookie Mix
1/2 C. butter or margarine,
  softened

2 eggs, slightly beaten
1 tsp. vanilla

Preheat the oven to 375°F. In a large bowl, cream the butter, eggs and vanilla. Remove the orange slice candies from the jar and set aside. Add the Orange Slice Cookie Mix and stir until the mixture is well blended. Stir in orange slice candies. Drop by rounded tablespoonfuls onto greased cookie sheet. Bake for 12 to 14 minutes. Transfer to wire racks to cool.

Orange Slice Cookies
Makes 3 to 4 dozen

1 jar Orange Slice Cookie Mix
1/2 C. butter or margarine,
  softened

2 eggs, slightly beaten
1 tsp. vanilla

Preheat the oven to 375°F. In a large bowl, cream the butter, eggs and vanilla. Remove the orange slice candies from the jar and set aside. Add the Orange Slice Cookie Mix and stir until the mixture is well blended. Stir in orange slice candies. Drop by rounded tablespoonfuls onto greased cookie sheet. Bake for 12 to 14 minutes. Transfer to wire racks to cool.

Orange Slice Cookies
Makes 3 to 4 dozen

1 jar Orange Slice Cookie Mix
1/2 C. butter or margarine,
  softened

2 eggs, slightly beaten
1 tsp. vanilla

Preheat the oven to 375°F. In a large bowl, cream the butter, eggs and vanilla. Remove the orange slice candies from the jar and set aside. Add the Orange Slice Cookie Mix and stir until the mixture is well blended. Stir in orange slice candies. Drop by rounded tablespoonfuls onto greased cookie sheet. Bake for 12 to 14 minutes. Transfer to wire racks to cool.

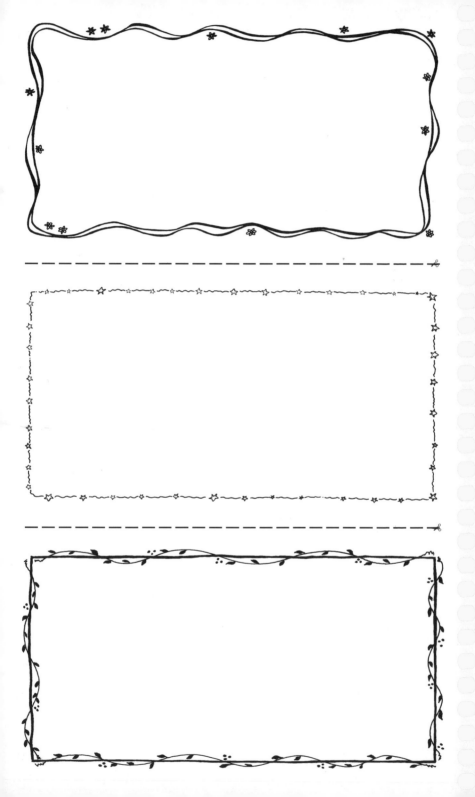

Orange Slice Cookies
Makes 3 to 4 dozen

1 jar Orange Slice Cookie Mix
1/2 C. butter or margarine, softened

2 eggs, slightly beaten
1 tsp. vanilla

Preheat the oven to 375°F. In a large bowl, cream the butter, eggs and vanilla. Remove the orange slice candies from the jar and set aside. Add the Orange Slice Cookie Mix and stir until the mixture is well blended. Stir in orange slice candies. Drop by rounded tablespoonfuls onto greased cookie sheet. Bake for 12 to 14 minutes. Transfer to wire racks to cool.

Orange Slice Cookies
Makes 3 to 4 dozen

1 jar Orange Slice Cookie Mix
1/2 C. butter or margarine, softened

2 eggs, slightly beaten
1 tsp. vanilla

Preheat the oven to 375°F. In a large bowl, cream the butter, eggs and vanilla. Remove the orange slice candies from the jar and set aside. Add the Orange Slice Cookie Mix and stir until the mixture is well blended. Stir in orange slice candies. Drop by rounded tablespoonfuls onto greased cookie sheet. Bake for 12 to 14 minutes. Transfer to wire racks to cool.

Orange Slice Cookies
Makes 3 to 4 dozen

1 jar Orange Slice Cookie Mix
1/2 C. butter or margarine, softened

2 eggs, slightly beaten
1 tsp. vanilla

Preheat the oven to 375°F. In a large bowl, cream the butter, eggs and vanilla. Remove the orange slice candies from the jar and set aside. Add the Orange Slice Cookie Mix and stir until the mixture is well blended. Stir in orange slice candies. Drop by rounded tablespoonfuls onto greased cookie sheet. Bake for 12 to 14 minutes. Transfer to wire racks to cool.

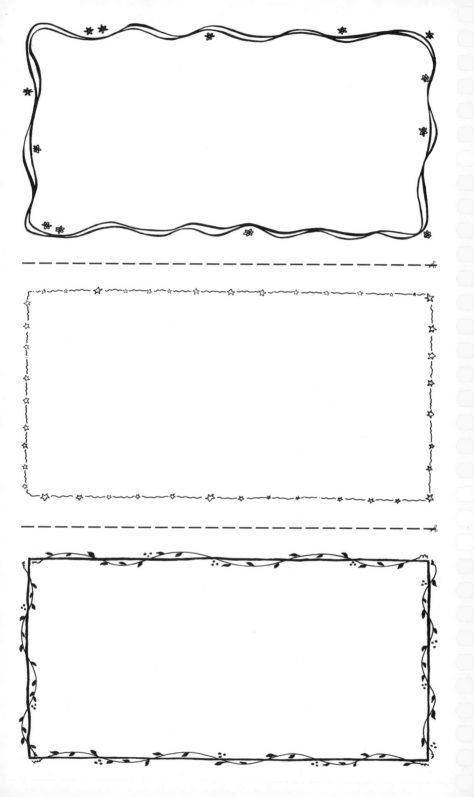

Peanut Butter Cookie Mix

3/4 C. chopped salted
   peanuts
3/4 C. brown sugar
3/4 C. sugar
1 1/2 C. all-purpose flour
1 tsp. baking soda
1 tsp. salt
3/4 C. peanut butter chips

Layer the ingredients in the order given into a wide-mouth 1-quart canning jar. Pack each layer in place before adding the next ingredient.

Attach a gift tag with the mixing and baking directions.

At times, it may seem impossible to make all of the jar ingredients fit, but with persistence, they do all fit.

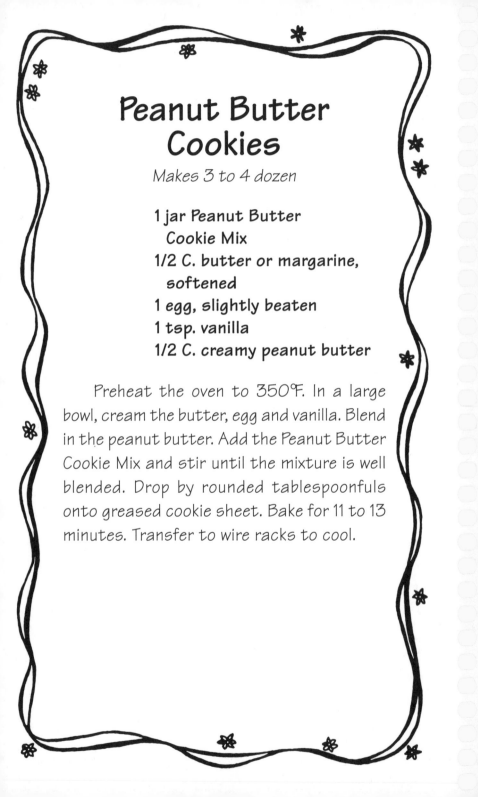

Peanut Butter Cookies

Makes 3 to 4 dozen

1 jar Peanut Butter
   Cookie Mix
1/2 C. butter or margarine,
   softened
1 egg, slightly beaten
1 tsp. vanilla
1/2 C. creamy peanut butter

Preheat the oven to 350°F. In a large bowl, cream the butter, egg and vanilla. Blend in the peanut butter. Add the Peanut Butter Cookie Mix and stir until the mixture is well blended. Drop by rounded tablespoonfuls onto greased cookie sheet. Bake for 11 to 13 minutes. Transfer to wire racks to cool.

Peanut Butter Cookies

Makes 3 to 4 dozen

1 jar Peanut Butter Cookie Mix
1/2 C. butter or margarine,
  softened

1 egg, slightly beaten
1 tsp. vanilla
1/2 C. creamy peanut butter

    Preheat the oven to 350°F. In a large bowl, cream the butter, egg and vanilla. Blend in the peanut butter. Add the Peanut Butter Cookie Mix and stir until the mixture is well blended. Drop by rounded tablespoonfuls onto greased cookie sheet. Bake for 11 to 13 minutes. Transfer to wire racks to cool.

Peanut Butter Cookies

Makes 3 to 4 dozen

1 jar Peanut Butter Cookie Mix
1/2 C. butter or margarine,
  softened

1 egg, slightly beaten
1 tsp. vanilla
1/2 C. creamy peanut butter

    Preheat the oven to 350°F. In a large bowl, cream the butter, egg and vanilla. Blend in the peanut butter. Add the Peanut Butter Cookie Mix and stir until the mixture is well blended. Drop by rounded tablespoonfuls onto greased cookie sheet. Bake for 11 to 13 minutes. Transfer to wire racks to cool.

Peanut Butter Cookies

Makes 3 to 4 dozen

1 jar Peanut Butter Cookie Mix
1/2 C. butter or margarine,
  softened

1 egg, slightly beaten
1 tsp. vanilla
1/2 C. creamy peanut butter

    Preheat the oven to 350°F. In a large bowl, cream the butter, egg and vanilla. Blend in the peanut butter. Add the Peanut Butter Cookie Mix and stir until the mixture is well blended. Drop by rounded tablespoonfuls onto greased cookie sheet. Bake for 11 to 13 minutes. Transfer to wire racks to cool.

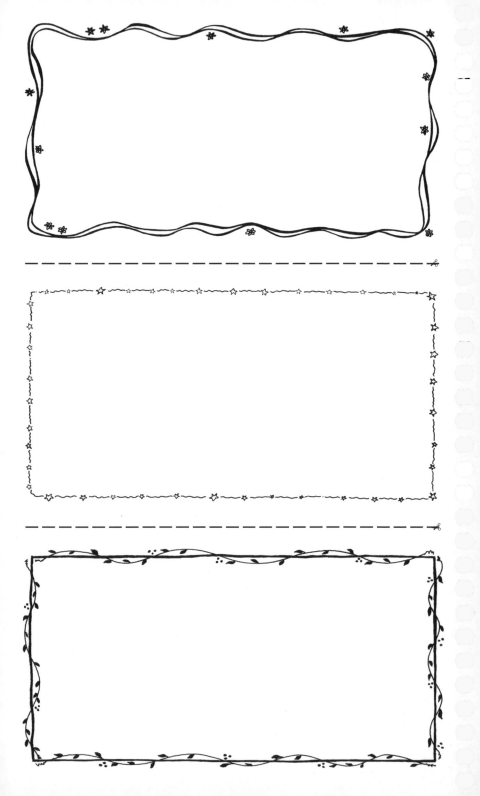

Peanut Butter Cookies
Makes 3 to 4 dozen

1 jar Peanut Butter Cookie Mix
1/2 C. butter or margarine,
  softened

1 egg, slightly beaten
1 tsp. vanilla
1/2 C. creamy peanut butter

Preheat the oven to 350°F. In a large bowl, cream the butter, egg and vanilla. Blend in the peanut butter. Add the Peanut Butter Cookie Mix and stir until the mixture is well blended. Drop by rounded tablespoonfuls onto greased cookie sheet. Bake for 11 to 13 minutes. Transfer to wire racks to cool.

Peanut Butter Cookies
Makes 3 to 4 dozen

1 jar Peanut Butter Cookie Mix
1/2 C. butter or margarine,
  softened

1 egg, slightly beaten
1 tsp. vanilla
1/2 C. creamy peanut butter

Preheat the oven to 350°F. In a large bowl, cream the butter, egg and vanilla. Blend in the peanut butter. Add the Peanut Butter Cookie Mix and stir until the mixture is well blended. Drop by rounded tablespoonfuls onto greased cookie sheet. Bake for 11 to 13 minutes. Transfer to wire racks to cool.

Peanut Butter Cookies
Makes 3 to 4 dozen

1 jar Peanut Butter Cookie Mix
1/2 C. butter or margarine,
  softened

1 egg, slightly beaten
1 tsp. vanilla
1/2 C. creamy peanut butter

Preheat the oven to 350°F. In a large bowl, cream the butter, egg and vanilla. Blend in the peanut butter. Add the Peanut Butter Cookie Mix and stir until the mixture is well blended. Drop by rounded tablespoonfuls onto greased cookie sheet. Bake for 11 to 13 minutes. Transfer to wire racks to cool.

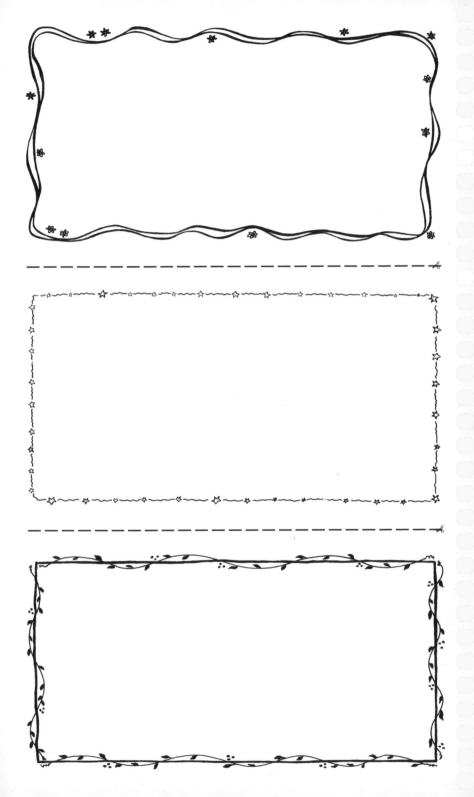

Raisin Crunch Cookie Mix

1/2 C. sugar
1/2 C. raisins
1 1/4 C. flaked coconut
1 C. cornflakes, crushed
3/4 C. brown sugar
1 1/4 C. all-purpose flour
1 tsp. baking soda
1 tsp. baking powder
1/2 C. quick oats

Layer the ingredients in the order given into a wide-mouth 1-quart canning jar. Pack each layer in place before adding the next ingredient.

Attach a gift tag with the mixing and baking directions.

❋ For an out of the ordinary gift, try placing the mix in a mixing bowl along with kitchen utensils, cookbooks, recipe cards, towels, potholders, and cookie cutters. ❋

Raisin Crunch Cookies

Makes 3 to 4 dozen

1 jar Raisin Crunch Cookie Mix
3/4 C. butter or margarine,
   softened
2 eggs, slightly beaten
1 tsp. vanilla

Preheat the oven to 350°F. In a large bowl, cream the butter, eggs and vanilla. Add the Raisin Crunch Cookie Mix and stir until the mixture is well blended. Drop by rounded tablespoonfuls onto greased cookie sheet. Bake for 10 to 12 minutes. Transfer to wire racks to cool.

Raisin Crunch Cookies
Makes 3 to 4 dozen

1 jar Raisin Crunch Cookie Mix
3/4 C. butter or margarine,
   softened

2 eggs, slightly beaten
1 tsp. vanilla

   Preheat the oven to 350°F. In a large bowl, cream the butter, eggs and vanilla. Add the Raisin Crunch Cookie Mix and stir until the mixture is well blended. Drop by rounded tablespoonfuls onto greased cookie sheet. Bake for 10 to 12 minutes. Transfer to wire racks to cool.

Raisin Crunch Cookies
Makes 3 to 4 dozen

1 jar Raisin Crunch Cookie Mix
3/4 C. butter or margarine,
   softened

2 eggs, slightly beaten
1 tsp. vanilla

   Preheat the oven to 350°F. In a large bowl, cream the butter, eggs and vanilla. Add the Raisin Crunch Cookie Mix and stir until the mixture is well blended. Drop by rounded tablespoonfuls onto greased cookie sheet. Bake for 10 to 12 minutes. Transfer to wire racks to cool.

Raisin Crunch Cookies
Makes 3 to 4 dozen

1 jar Raisin Crunch Cookie Mix
3/4 C. butter or margarine,
   softened

2 eggs, slightly beaten
1 tsp. vanilla

   Preheat the oven to 350°F. In a large bowl, cream the butter, eggs and vanilla. Add the Raisin Crunch Cookie Mix and stir until the mixture is well blended. Drop by rounded tablespoonfuls onto greased cookie sheet. Bake for 10 to 12 minutes. Transfer to wire racks to cool.

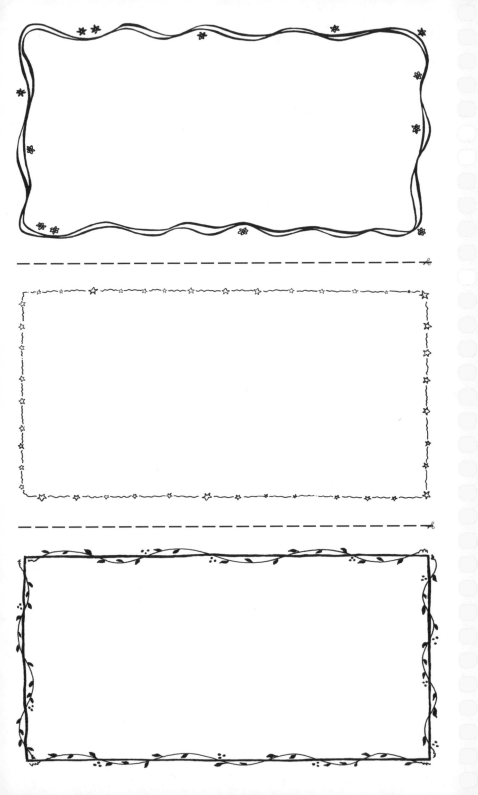

Raisin Crunch Cookies
Makes 3 to 4 dozen

1 jar Raisin Crunch Cookie Mix
3/4 C. butter or margarine,
softened

2 eggs, slightly beaten
1 tsp. vanilla

Preheat the oven to 350°F. In a large bowl, cream the butter, eggs and vanilla. Add the Raisin Crunch Cookie Mix and stir until the mixture is well blended. Drop by rounded tablespoonfuls onto greased cookie sheet. Bake for 10 to 12 minutes. Transfer to wire racks to cool.

Raisin Crunch Cookies
Makes 3 to 4 dozen

1 jar Raisin Crunch Cookie Mix
3/4 C. butter or margarine,
softened

2 eggs, slightly beaten
1 tsp. vanilla

Preheat the oven to 350°F. In a large bowl, cream the butter, eggs and vanilla. Add the Raisin Crunch Cookie Mix and stir until the mixture is well blended. Drop by rounded tablespoonfuls onto greased cookie sheet. Bake for 10 to 12 minutes. Transfer to wire racks to cool.

Raisin Crunch Cookies
Makes 3 to 4 dozen

1 jar Raisin Crunch Cookie Mix
3/4 C. butter or margarine,
softened

2 eggs, slightly beaten
1 tsp. vanilla

Preheat the oven to 350°F. In a large bowl, cream the butter, eggs and vanilla. Add the Raisin Crunch Cookie Mix and stir until the mixture is well blended. Drop by rounded tablespoonfuls onto greased cookie sheet. Bake for 10 to 12 minutes. Transfer to wire racks to cool.

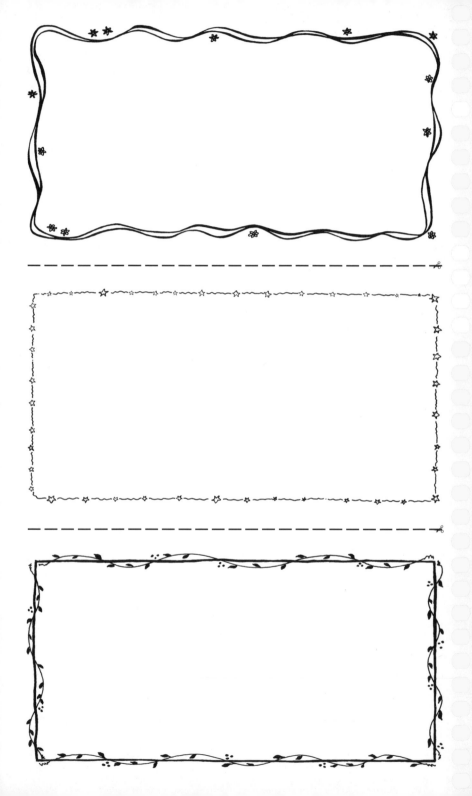

Chocolate Covered Raisin Cookie Mix

3/4 C. sugar
1 C. chocolate covered raisins
1/2 C. milk chocolate chips
1/2 C. brown sugar
2 C. all-purpose flour
1 tsp. baking powder
1 tsp. salt

Layer the ingredients in the order given into a wide-mouth 1-quart canning jar. Pack each layer in place before adding the next ingredient.

Attach a gift tag with the mixing and baking directions.

❀ *Small appliques or embroidery can be added to the center of a fabric cover to further personalize the gift.* ❀

Chocolate Covered Raisin Cookies

Makes 3 to 4 dozen

1 jar Chocolate Covered Raisin
    Cookie Mix
1/2 C. butter or margarine,
    softened
2 eggs, slightly beaten
1 tsp. vanilla

Preheat the oven to 375°F. In a large bowl, cream the butter, eggs and vanilla. Add the Chocolate Covered Raisin Cookie Mix and stir until the mixture is well blended. Drop by rounded tablespoonfuls onto greased cookie sheet. Bake for 10 to 13 minutes. Transfer to wire racks to cool.

Chocolate Covered Raisin Cookies
Makes 3 to 4 dozen

1 jar Chocolate Covered Raisin
  Cookie Mix
1/2 C. butter or margarine,
  softened

2 eggs, slightly beaten
1 tsp. vanilla

Preheat the oven to 375°F. In a large bowl, cream the butter, eggs and vanilla. Add the Chocolate Covered Raisin Cookie Mix and stir until the mixture is well blended. Drop by rounded tablespoonfuls onto greased cookie sheet. Bake for 10 to 13 minutes. Transfer to wire racks to cool.

Chocolate Covered Raisin Cookies
Makes 3 to 4 dozen

1 jar Chocolate Covered Raisin
  Cookie Mix
1/2 C. butter or margarine,
  softened

2 eggs, slightly beaten
1 tsp. vanilla

Preheat the oven to 375°F. In a large bowl, cream the butter, eggs and vanilla. Add the Chocolate Covered Raisin Cookie Mix and stir until the mixture is well blended. Drop by rounded tablespoonfuls onto greased cookie sheet. Bake for 10 to 13 minutes. Transfer to wire racks to cool.

Chocolate Covered Raisin Cookies
Makes 3 to 4 dozen

1 jar Chocolate Covered Raisin
  Cookie Mix
1/2 C. butter or margarine,
  softened

2 eggs, slightly beaten
1 tsp. vanilla

Preheat the oven to 375°F. In a large bowl, cream the butter, eggs and vanilla. Add the Chocolate Covered Raisin Cookie Mix and stir until the mixture is well blended. Drop by rounded tablespoonfuls onto greased cookie sheet. Bake for 10 to 13 minutes. Transfer to wire racks to cool.

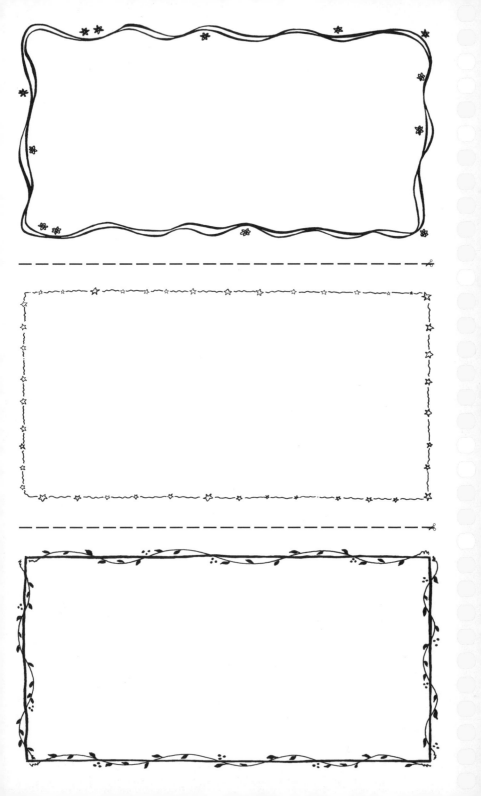

Chocolate Covered Raisin Cookies
Makes 3 to 4 dozen

1 jar Chocolate Covered Raisin
  Cookie Mix
1/2 C. butter or margarine,
  softened

2 eggs, slightly beaten
1 tsp. vanilla

Preheat the oven to 375°F. In a large bowl, cream the butter, eggs and vanilla. Add the Chocolate Covered Raisin Cookie Mix and stir until the mixture is well blended. Drop by rounded tablespoonfuls onto greased cookie sheet. Bake for 10 to 13 minutes. Transfer to wire racks to cool.

Chocolate Covered Raisin Cookies
Makes 3 to 4 dozen

1 jar Chocolate Covered Raisin
  Cookie Mix
1/2 C. butter or margarine,
  softened

2 eggs, slightly beaten
1 tsp. vanilla

Preheat the oven to 375°F. In a large bowl, cream the butter, eggs and vanilla. Add the Chocolate Covered Raisin Cookie Mix and stir until the mixture is well blended. Drop by rounded tablespoonfuls onto greased cookie sheet. Bake for 10 to 13 minutes. Transfer to wire racks to cool.

Chocolate Covered Raisin Cookies
Makes 3 to 4 dozen

1 jar Chocolate Covered Raisin
  Cookie Mix
1/2 C. butter or margarine,
  softened

2 eggs, slightly beaten
1 tsp. vanilla

Preheat the oven to 375°F. In a large bowl, cream the butter, eggs and vanilla. Add the Chocolate Covered Raisin Cookie Mix and stir until the mixture is well blended. Drop by rounded tablespoonfuls onto greased cookie sheet. Bake for 10 to 13 minutes. Transfer to wire racks to cool.

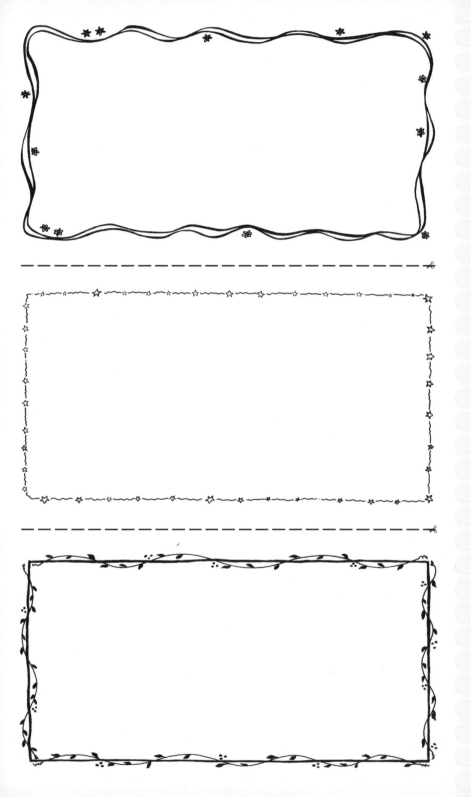

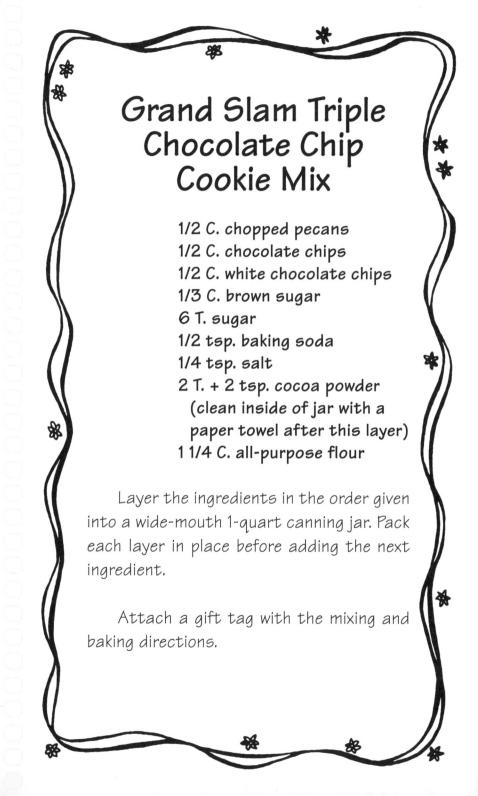

Grand Slam Triple Chocolate Chip Cookie Mix

1/2 C. chopped pecans
1/2 C. chocolate chips
1/2 C. white chocolate chips
1/3 C. brown sugar
6 T. sugar
1/2 tsp. baking soda
1/4 tsp. salt
2 T. + 2 tsp. cocoa powder
   (clean inside of jar with a
   paper towel after this layer)
1 1/4 C. all-purpose flour

Layer the ingredients in the order given into a wide-mouth 1-quart canning jar. Pack each layer in place before adding the next ingredient.

Attach a gift tag with the mixing and baking directions.

Grand Slam Triple Chocolate Chip Cookies

Makes 3 to 4 dozen

1 jar Grand Slam Triple
   Chocolate Chip Cookie Mix
1/2 C. butter or margarine,
   softened
2 eggs, slightly beaten
1 T. milk
1 tsp. vanilla

Preheat the oven to 350°F. In a large bowl, cream the butter, eggs, milk and vanilla. Add the Grand Slam Triple Chocolate Chip Cookie Mix and stir until the mixture is well blended. Drop by rounded tablespoonfuls onto greased cookie sheet. Bake for 8 to 10 minutes. Transfer to wire racks to cool.

Grand Slam Triple Chocolate Chip Cookies
Makes 3 to 4 dozen

1 jar Grand Slam Triple
  Chocolate Chip Cookie Mix
1/2 C. butter or margarine,
  softened

2 eggs, slightly beaten
1 T. milk
1 tsp. vanilla

Preheat the oven to 350°F. In a large bowl, cream the butter, eggs, milk and vanilla. Add the Grand Slam Triple Chocolate Chip Cookie Mix and stir until the mixture is well blended. Drop by rounded tablespoonfuls onto greased cookie sheet. Bake for 8 to 10 minutes. Transfer to wire racks to cool.

Grand Slam Triple Chocolate Chip Cookies
Makes 3 to 4 dozen

1 jar Grand Slam Triple
  Chocolate Chip Cookie Mix
1/2 C. butter or margarine,
  softened

2 eggs, slightly beaten
1 T. milk
1 tsp. vanilla

Preheat the oven to 350°F. In a large bowl, cream the butter, eggs, milk and vanilla. Add the Grand Slam Triple Chocolate Chip Cookie Mix and stir until the mixture is well blended. Drop by rounded tablespoonfuls onto greased cookie sheet. Bake for 8 to 10 minutes. Transfer to wire racks to cool.

Grand Slam Triple Chocolate Chip Cookies
Makes 3 to 4 dozen

1 jar Grand Slam Triple
  Chocolate Chip Cookie Mix
1/2 C. butter or margarine,
  softened

2 eggs, slightly beaten
1 T. milk
1 tsp. vanilla

Preheat the oven to 350°F. In a large bowl, cream the butter, eggs, milk and vanilla. Add the Grand Slam Triple Chocolate Chip Cookie Mix and stir until the mixture is well blended. Drop by rounded tablespoonfuls onto greased cookie sheet. Bake for 8 to 10 minutes. Transfer to wire racks to cool.

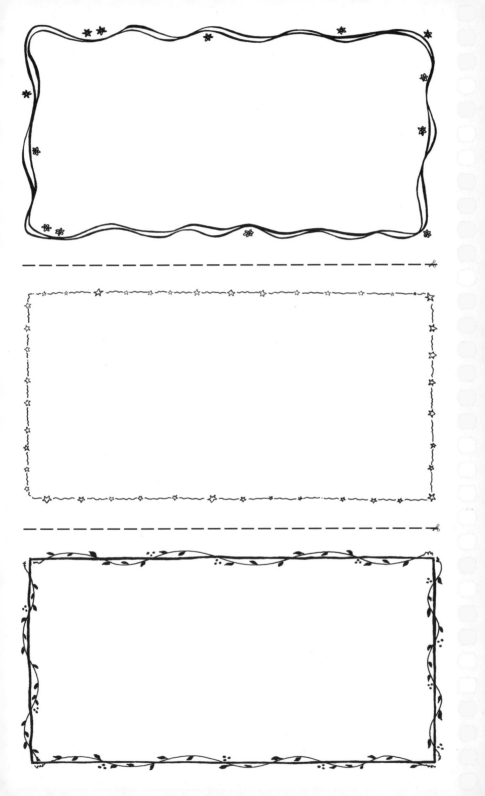

Grand Slam Triple Chocolate Chip Cookies
Makes 3 to 4 dozen

1 jar Grand Slam Triple
   Chocolate Chip Cookie Mix
1/2 C. butter or margarine,
   softened

2 eggs, slightly beaten
1 T. milk
1 tsp. vanilla

Preheat the oven to 350°F. In a large bowl, cream the butter, eggs, milk and vanilla. Add the Grand Slam Triple Chocolate Chip Cookie Mix and stir until the mixture is well blended. Drop by rounded tablespoonfuls onto greased cookie sheet. Bake for 8 to 10 minutes. Transfer to wire racks to cool.

Grand Slam Triple Chocolate Chip Cookies
Makes 3 to 4 dozen

1 jar Grand Slam Triple
   Chocolate Chip Cookie Mix
1/2 C. butter or margarine,
   softened

2 eggs, slightly beaten
1 T. milk
1 tsp. vanilla

Preheat the oven to 350°F. In a large bowl, cream the butter, eggs, milk and vanilla. Add the Grand Slam Triple Chocolate Chip Cookie Mix and stir until the mixture is well blended. Drop by rounded tablespoonfuls onto greased cookie sheet. Bake for 8 to 10 minutes. Transfer to wire racks to cool.

Grand Slam Triple Chocolate Chip Cookies
Makes 3 to 4 dozen

1 jar Grand Slam Triple
   Chocolate Chip Cookie Mix
1/2 C. butter or margarine,
   softened

2 eggs, slightly beaten
1 T. milk
1 tsp. vanilla

Preheat the oven to 350°F. In a large bowl, cream the butter, eggs, milk and vanilla. Add the Grand Slam Triple Chocolate Chip Cookie Mix and stir until the mixture is well blended. Drop by rounded tablespoonfuls onto greased cookie sheet. Bake for 8 to 10 minutes. Transfer to wire racks to cool.

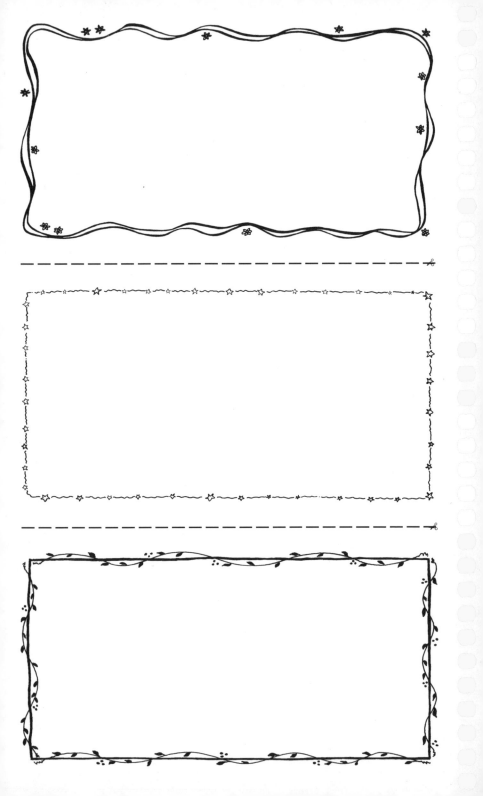

Gourmet Cookie Mix

1 C. all-purpose flour
1/2 tsp. baking powder
1/2 tsp. baking soda
1 1/4 C. old-fashioned oats,
   blended
1 (5.5 ounce) milk chocolate bar,
   grated
1/2 C. sugar
1/2 C. brown sugar
1/2 C. chopped nuts, your choice
   (optional)
1/2 C. chocolate chips

Layer the ingredients in the order given into a wide-mouth 1-quart canning jar. Pack each layer in place before adding the next ingredient.

Attach a gift tag with the mixing and baking directions.

❀ For a special touch, attach a cookie cutter or wooden spoon to the jar. ❀

Gourmet Cookies

Makes 3 to 4 dozen

1 jar Gourmet Cookie Mix
1/2 C. butter or margarine,
   softened
2 eggs, slightly beaten
1 T. milk
1 tsp. vanilla

Preheat the oven to 350°F. In a large bowl, cream the butter, eggs, milk and vanilla. Add the Gourmet Cookie Mix and stir until the mixture is well blended. Drop by rounded tablespoonfuls onto greased cookie sheet. Bake for 8 to 10 minutes. Transfer to wire racks to cool.

Gourmet Cookies
Makes 3 to 4 dozen

1 jar Gourmet Cookie Mix
1/2 C. butter or margarine,
  softened

2 eggs, slightly beaten
1 T. milk
1 tsp. vanilla

    Preheat the oven to 350°F. In a large bowl, cream the butter, eggs, milk and vanilla. Add the Gourmet Cookie Mix and stir until the mixture is well blended. Drop by rounded tablespoonfuls onto greased cookie sheet. Bake for 8 to 10 minutes. Transfer to wire racks to cool.

Gourmet Cookies
Makes 3 to 4 dozen

1 jar Gourmet Cookie Mix
1/2 C. butter or margarine,
  softened

2 eggs, slightly beaten
1 T. milk
1 tsp. vanilla

    Preheat the oven to 350°F. In a large bowl, cream the butter, eggs, milk and vanilla. Add the Gourmet Cookie Mix and stir until the mixture is well blended. Drop by rounded tablespoonfuls onto greased cookie sheet. Bake for 8 to 10 minutes. Transfer to wire racks to cool.

Gourmet Cookies
Makes 3 to 4 dozen

1 jar Gourmet Cookie Mix
1/2 C. butter or margarine,
  softened

2 eggs, slightly beaten
1 T. milk
1 tsp. vanilla

    Preheat the oven to 350°F. In a large bowl, cream the butter, eggs, milk and vanilla. Add the Gourmet Cookie Mix and stir until the mixture is well blended. Drop by rounded tablespoonfuls onto greased cookie sheet. Bake for 8 to 10 minutes. Transfer to wire racks to cool.

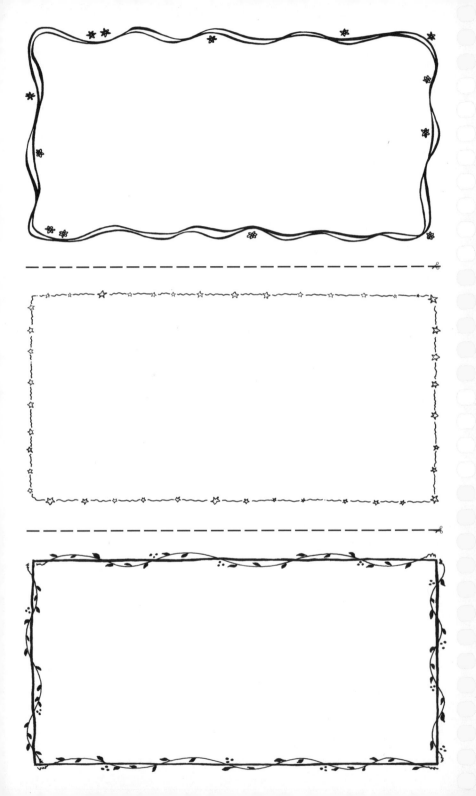

Gourmet Cookies
Makes 3 to 4 dozen

1 jar Gourmet Cookie Mix
1/2 C. butter or margarine,
  softened

2 eggs, slightly beaten
1 T. milk
1 tsp. vanilla

Preheat the oven to 350°F. In a large bowl, cream the butter, eggs, milk and vanilla. Add the Gourmet Cookie Mix and stir until the mixture is well blended. Drop by rounded tablespoonfuls onto greased cookie sheet. Bake for 8 to 10 minutes. Transfer to wire racks to cool.

Gourmet Cookies
Makes 3 to 4 dozen

1 jar Gourmet Cookie Mix
1/2 C. butter or margarine,
  softened

2 eggs, slightly beaten
1 T. milk
1 tsp. vanilla

Preheat the oven to 350°F. In a large bowl, cream the butter, eggs, milk and vanilla. Add the Gourmet Cookie Mix and stir until the mixture is well blended. Drop by rounded tablespoonfuls onto greased cookie sheet. Bake for 8 to 10 minutes. Transfer to wire racks to cool.

Gourmet Cookies
Makes 3 to 4 dozen

1 jar Gourmet Cookie Mix
1/2 C. butter or margarine,
  softened

2 eggs, slightly beaten
1 T. milk
1 tsp. vanilla

Preheat the oven to 350°F. In a large bowl, cream the butter, eggs, milk and vanilla. Add the Gourmet Cookie Mix and stir until the mixture is well blended. Drop by rounded tablespoonfuls onto greased cookie sheet. Bake for 8 to 10 minutes. Transfer to wire racks to cool.

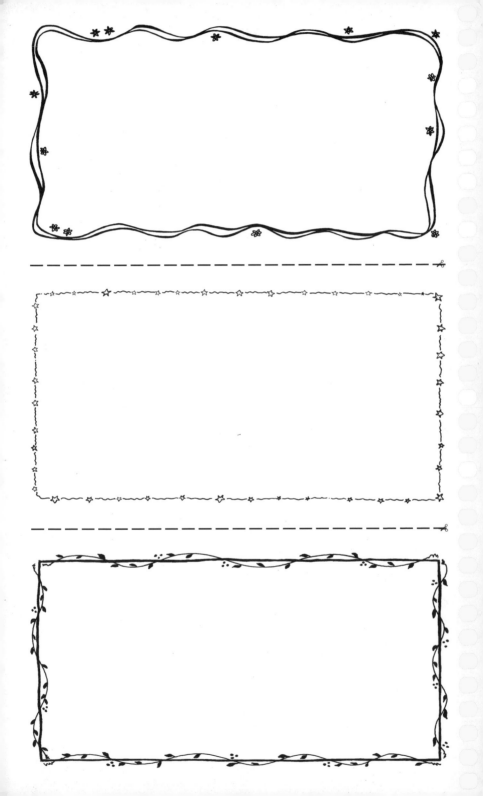